EVERYONE
LOVES
A
GOOD
TRAIN WRECK

Against Happiness: In Praise of Melancholy

EVERYONE LOVES A GOOD TRAIN WRECK

Why We Can't Look Away

ERIC G. WILSON

SARAH CRICHTON BOOKS

Farrar, Straus and Giroux | *New York*

Sarah Crichton Books
Farrar, Straus and Giroux
18 West 18th Street, New York 10011

Printed in the United States of America
First edition, 2012

Library of Congress Cataloging-in-Publication Data
Wilson, Eric, 1967–
    Everyone loves a good train wreck : why we can't look
away / Eric G. Wilson.—1st ed.
       p.   cm.
    ISBN 978-0-374-15033-4 (alk. paper)
    1. Curiosity.   2. Disasters—Psychological aspects.
3. Horror—Social aspects.   I. Title.

BF323.C8W55 2012
155.9'35—dc23

                       2011034954

Designed by Abby Kagan

www.fsgbooks.com

P 1

05 17

TO KIRK, MY BROTHER,

who turned me on to horror movies

The sinister, the terrible never deceive: the state in which they leave us is always one of enlightenment. —THOMAS LIGOTTI

Violence and smut are of course everywhere on the airwaves. You cannot turn on your television without seeing them, although sometimes you have to hunt around. —DAVE BARRY

The goal of all life is death. —SIGMUND FREUD

EVERYONE
LOVES
A
GOOD
TRAIN WRECK

1.

"Don't look."

That's what she asked, more than once. I heard her distinctly each time, and told myself I should oblige, and even once partially turned my head in her direction, but I just couldn't take my eyes off the screen. I engrossed myself again, and again submitted to the anger, the sorrow, the fear, as well as guilt's perverse pleasure: I felt that I shouldn't be doing this, but I was doing it anyway, and got a peevish thrill from my transgression.

It was evening, dinnertime, and this had been going on since morning, right before I left for work. I had just finished breakfast. I had my satchel over my shoulder. It contained my books for that day's class (on Keats's "To Autumn") and also my lunch (a peanut butter sandwich). I had my hand on the doorknob, ready to leave, when Sandi, my wife, ran up to me, phone in hand, and said, "Turn on the TV."

I did, and there it was. Too slowly, a jet, brilliant white, wide enough to seat a hundred, plowed into a narrow rectangular tower, luminous and silver in the September sunshine. The blast silently boomed, and the skyscraper turned black billow, spume of flame: an immense sinister candle.

There was a stop, and the sequence rolled once more, soundless, with the same dilatory tempo. It repeated, each time more mesmerizing and meaningless, someone else's eerie dream. No words explained it—fit it into a familiar story, with reassuring causalities and characters. It was unmoored destruction, sublime. I watched, and watched.

We all know what this was, and likely remember our need to witness the eruption one more time, and also to look when the events became more horrific: another fiery collision, and then buildings sucked to the ground, leaving only rubble and crushed loved ones.

Sandi's voice broke my morbid trance that morning: "Come here." When I faced her, she appeared to me in the fullness of her three-month pregnancy, holding in her smooth belly a little creature who would soon be pressed from the warm darkness into this glare.

We hugged, not confessing our terror: an infant in this Armageddon. We sat down together and watched the catastrophe worsen.

After an hour, I made my way to my office at the university where I teach. I had seen the attacks on the towers probably twenty times by then. I turned on my computer, went to the Internet, and found the scene again.

But I had classes to teach, and so reluctantly left the screen. I held the students only briefly in each of my three sections, telling them that we would pick up with Keats the next class— even his wisdom did not that day suffice—and urging them to go back to their dorms and call their families and friends.

Between classes, I persisted in watching the footage, breaking only to call Sandi, to comfort and in turn take solace.

I returned home around five. Sandi was in the kitchen preparing dinner, food that would best nourish our baby. The small television beside the coffeemaker, like the other sets in our house, was off.

After giving my wife a hug, I clicked the set on: the conflagration in the sky, now strangely comforting, like a wound you can't imagine not having. More than that, the footage at this point was, as shocking as this might sound, gruesomely beautiful: swelling ebony smoke against the blue horizon. And the film inspired this staggering thought: "Here is one of those rare ruptures from which history will not recover, and I am alive at its occurrence." I felt exhilarated, inappropriately, and I was ashamed.

"Come on," Sandi said. "Turn it off and help me chop the vegetables. Don't look."

But I did, though she asked me again to stop, and I continued into the night, brooding.

2.

Don't look. Look. This refrain has played in my head much of my life, one voice telling me it's wrong to stare at morbid events and another urging me to stare anyway, hard.

It's my turn to pass the accident on the side of the highway. I tell myself to keep my eyes on the road, to avoid being one of those rubberneckers who clog traffic just for some sick titillation. But decadent anticipation takes over; I realize I'm going to gaze, and I'll enjoy the experience all the more because it's frowned upon. I hit my brakes and gape, until an angry horn prods me forward.

In high school, I heard there was a fight behind the cafeteria. I hurried along with everyone else to see it. Elbowing classmates aside to get a better view, I felt shame mixed with excitement. Here was something savage, but also vital, one boy mauling another.

In both cases, and there have been many others, there was a compulsion to watch, like that tickle in the throat, followed by the irrepressible cough, or the awful urge to sneeze: once it activates, it's impossible to contain. The only good of holding back is that it makes the imminent release more intense.

I imagine we've all felt that guilty rush before the morbid. The exploitation of a suicidal starlet, the assassination of a world leader; the hypnotic crush of a hurricane, the lion exploding into the antelope; the wreckage and the rapture, the profane and the sacred: whatever our attraction, we are drawn to doom.

Everyone loves a good train wreck. We are enamored of ruin. The deeper the darkness is, the more dazzling. Our secret and ecstatic wish: Let it all fall down.

Our modern, enlightened parents probably encouraged us to worship wholesome heroes and sunshine. They taught us to avoid the lurid. In the gloom—there lurks sin. Stay away from dead things.

But the corpse once had its day. In fact, "separation of death from everyday life," as the historian Gary Laderman put it, is a fairly recent development. Up until the early years of the last century, people usually suffered and died in their own homes. Adults and children alike were intimate with death—its sounds and its smells, the agony of it, and its peace. Since the 1950s, though, the health-care industry has increasingly taken charge of death, as well as birth. Now—enticed by well-trained doctors, sophisticated medical technologies, and spotless rooms—almost everyone, understandably, goes to the hospital to die.

Or not. The medical establishment holds out this desperate hope: The good doctor, at any cost, will keep you alive. Here's how the historian Philippe Ariès describes this fantasy. In the last century "[d]eath . . . ceased to be accepted as a natural, necessary phenomenon. Death is [now] a failure, a 'business lost.'

This is . . . the attitude of the doctor, who claims the control of death as his mission in life. But the doctor is merely the spokesman for society. When death arrives, it is regarded as an accident, a sign of helplessness and clumsiness that must be put out of the mind."

The hospital hides the morbid, the macabre. The funeral home does, too. When the doctor bitterly loses his battle with the reaper, the mortician manages the damage. He shields us from the corruption. Through embalming, he slows the cadaver's decay. He places the body in a handsome coffin that resembles a bed more than a receptacle of guts. And he prettifies the face so that it almost looks alive.

Most don't just abhor the corpse, but loathe all rot. Used to be, we might conclude our lunch of Kentucky Fried Chicken, a whole greasy box full, by wiping our hands with that damp, hygienic-smelling little paper towel provided in our packet of plastic utensils (including the "spork"). Now we glop our palms with hand sanitizer twenty times a day, bent on killing all those pathogens. Antibacterial soaps and antibiotics crowd our bathrooms. Plastic surgery—a war on decay—is becoming de rigueur.

But to battle death is to lose the feeling of life. What the biologist Lynn Margulis says about our fear of putrefaction can apply to our unease toward all things morbid: "When you advocate your soaps that say they kill all harmful bacteria, you are committing suicide." Bacteria keep our blood pumping. In the words of Burkhard Bilger, who wrote an article on the nutritional value of fermentation, microbes "process the nutrients in our guts, produce chemicals that trigger sleep, ferment the sweat on our skin and the glucose in our muscles . . . They work with the immune system to mediate common infections. Even our own cells are kept alive by mitochondria."

The body's blights are exactly what make it work. This biological fact translates to a more existential one: to shut our eyes to corpses—to those around us now and to the particular one that each of us will become—is to blind ourselves to an integral part of a vibrant existence. Though we frequently ignore death or hide it in the haze of euphemism, we know, in our bones, this stark truth: Just as winter reveals the power of spring, closeness to death discloses our most fertile energies. We are reminded of our brief time on this earth, and feel inspired to make the most of it.

Maybe this is why so many of us are morbid, secretly or not, among the disinfectants and the plastics. We secretly hate Purell. Deep down, we know who we are: the cadaver as much as the creature; vampires, more or less.

I am an English professor obsessed with the Gothic worlds of Coleridge and Poe, Dickinson and Keats (though I rarely wear black, and hate emo songs). I have published a book on the limitations of happiness and the powers of melancholy. (I wish it had made Oprah's uplifting list.) I've written a memoir—no parenthetical wryness here—on my own struggles with devastating depression. But I remain in the dark when it comes to why I was drawn to the morbid, for better or worse, in the first place, and why so many others have felt the attraction, too.

This is my terra incognita: the origin of morbid curiosity, its nature, and how it works. There are maps in existence already, and I will use them as best I can, drawing on the findings of biologists, sociologists, psychologists, anthropologists, philosophers, theologians, and artists. Combining these with my own experience, I hope to illuminate the dark heart of so many of our most profound encounters, as well as the black comedy that makes us grin through the grimace: both the pulse and snicker that have animated not only Poe and Dickinson but also Melville, Hawthorne, Georgia O'Keeffe, Houdini, Ralph Ellison, the Louvin Brothers, Tod Browning, Chaplin, Faulkner, Buster Keaton, William Burroughs, Flannery O'Connor, Sylvia Plath, Anne Sexton, Lenny Bruce, Andy Kaufman, Laurie Anderson, Bob Dylan, Toni Morrison, and David Lynch. And these are only a few of those "pure products of America," to invoke William Carlos Williams, whose craziness holds us and won't let go.

4.

"Don't generalize; you can't speak for everyone." I'm weary of inscribing this criticism, in ink red as blood, into the margins of my students' compositions. But here I am doing that very thing, using the pronoun "we" to refer to collective humanity. I suppose I get a C. This grammar is of course problematic because it assumes that everyone is, on some level, the same, and thus overlooks this obvious and important fact: Differences in gender, age, class, race, history, and thousands of other factors make homogeneity impossible.

I should be more sympathetic to my students. They're straining to get from their "I" to the collective "we," and why not? Isn't this one of our great human needs, however misguided: to find unity between our personal experience and the lives of others? I'm certainly trying to make the connection in this book.

Forgive me, then, if I generalize from time to time. Yes, it's wrong to assume that everyone is morbidly curious, and that morbid curiosity takes the same form across space and time. Still, it's also quite apparent that I'm far from alone in my fascination with the morbid: macabre voyeurism is pervasive, and has been for centuries, and is in fact, as we'll see in the course of this book, much more common than we probably realize. And it may well be that we experience death and violence in deeply similar ways. Our addiction to the grim is perhaps our common ground.

In this book, I oscillate between personal confession and general analysis, with each side informing and transforming the other. My hope is that you'll close the book less with a smooth maxim and more with a fulfilling, thought-provoking response to two of life's greatest, most pressing and persistent questions: What is the meaning of suffering? What is the significance of death?

This is all I can promise: I will guide you, as best I can, into the rich depths of these questions. Other inquiries—some serious, others mordant—will mark our way. What can elephants tell us about the macabre? Do all children like to blow things up? Should you sleep in a coffin? How is Jesus like a serial killer? What's wrong with Saturn eating his child? Is staring at skulls wise? When does a site of wreckage, where lost loved ones are buried, become holy ground?

5.

Why am I so interested in the morbid? It is impossible to locate clear causes for our obsessions—are they genetic, environmental, results of our own choices, or all three combined?—but our personal histories do bear what Wordsworth calls "spots of time," those moments, often painful and pleasurable at once, that reveal depths we didn't know we had. These moments alter our interiors and continue for years afterward to nourish our souls. And so we nostalgically long for these spells, sensing that within their durations we were, fully and vividly, *alive.*

I am sixteen years old and standing in our dank basement, saved from total blackness only by one dingy window. I'm down here for one reason—to mock my little brother's movie.

For the past two years of his life—he's now twelve—he's watched every horror movie he could rent from the local video store. The older ones—the classic Universals from the 1930s, like *Frankenstein* and *Dracula*, as well as the creepy, crimson Hammer remakes from the '60s—he has viewed with my parents' permission. But he has also found a way, usually at the more lenient households of friends, to take in the gore fests of the early '80s—the *Friday the 13th* and the *Nightmare on Elm Street* series, and total junk like *Satan's Cheerleaders* and *Motel Hell*. The boy is addicted to horror, as is his best friend. When his buddy gets a used 8 mm camera for his birthday, they decide to make their own scary movie.

I think their obsession with horror is ridiculous—perverse wallowing in lowbrow trash. I am devoted, I tell myself, to worthier, more normal pursuits—athletics, namely (I'm the starting quarterback), but also the Beatles and J. D. Salinger.

But here I am, in the cold, moldy basement, waiting for my brother's friend to set up the projector. I'm sure that what I'm about to see will be laughably bad. During the movie's making, I glimpsed scenes riotously funny, in spite of themselves: a fat neighborhood kid in a rubber pig mask trying to hide behind a thin pine tree; ketchup mixed with water splattered on my parents' old gray canvas tent; another of my brother's friends fake-screaming as he stumbles barefoot through a field.

The light from the projector flows to the white sheet hanging on the cinder-block wall. A black-and-white image appears: the pig face. Muted by shade, silent, grainy, quivering in the frame of the handheld camera, it's not funny. It's unearthly, like an August fever's reverie: half-closed blinds, afternoon sunlight feeling deadly. A monstrous snout protrudes under squinty, empty eyes.

A harsh brightness, as if someone threw the camera into the sun, and then three tree trunks. Something rushes through the frame: a human. Another follows. Stops. It is the pig man, and he holds an axe. There's a glare again, and a fire appears. On the ground around it are four boys, their heads down. The axe is in the air; down it chops. A blackish fluid flickers and a round thing with hair rolls over the leaves. Dark goes the screen.

My brother and his friend break into laughter. They yell that their film sucks immensely. This *is* a movie, I remind myself, a dumb, terrible movie. But it's dredging up strange desires I've been afraid to express, even admit. Like how I want to shut myself in my dim bedroom all day, hidden from the judging looks of teachers and coaches. Like how, in this murkiness, I want to imagine disturbing pictures that would scare my dad into calling the doctor: myself dead in a coffin, for instance, with people I don't know hovering above.

I know my brother, now mocking his movie in a made-up song, can't know about these feelings, but I become self-conscious anyway, embarrassed. I shake my head, and then do what most boys would do. I turn to my brother and his friend, and I say, "That was stupid. I've got better things to do. I'm going to work out."

I walk out of the basement and into our white linoleum kitchen and then into my room, which smells of sweaty socks. I open the window and change into gym clothes and resolve to bench-press more than I ever have before.

_6._

Soon after that uncanny experience, though, I abandoned the gym for Weird Town. I sought out my dark room and the disturbing fantasies it produced. I read the disquieting parables of Kafka. I fell into Poe's labyrinths. I listened obsessively to Springsteen's _Nebraska_, with its wasted cornfields and broken wanderers. I wrote lyrics of my own, surreal and quite ridiculous, usually involving rats. I risked becoming a parody of teen angst. (Bart Simpson once said, upon hearing a Smashing Pumpkins song, "Making teenagers depressed is like shooting fish in a barrel.")

Thus began the awkward split—one that most of us suffer—between socially acceptable façade and interior strangeness. The exterior is a useful mask, necessary for survival and success. Those lacking such an appearance are misanthropes, losers, or lunatics. But we all understand, those times we are honest, late on an insomniac night, the limits of the veil. The engrossing action is inside, where our appetites run rampant: lust for power and erotic pleasure, fantasies of failure and sometimes death.

Poe calls this urge for destruction the "imp of the perverse." Imagine, he asks, standing on the brink of a precipice. "We peer into the abyss—we grow sick and dizzy. Our first impulse is to shrink from the danger. Unaccountably we remain." The more our reason "violently deters us from the brink . . . the more we impetuously approach it. There is no passion in nature so demoniacally impatient as that of him, who shuddering upon the edge of a precipice, thus meditates a plunge." This unsettling scene and the many that resemble it—yelling profanity at a funeral, being tempted by the one mistake that will wreck our careers—arise from the "spirit of the *Perverse*," the hunger to do exactly what we should not.

The battle between reasonableness and delinquency is the likely source of our fascination with split personalities. Mr. Hyde bedevils Dr. Jekyll. The attic picture of his hideous sins troubles beautiful Dorian Gray. Batman is the dark double of Bruce Wayne, as Spider-Man is of Peter Parker. We see ourselves mirrored in these cracked characters. We fantasize about a separate life, hidden, in which we can indulge our destructive obsessions.

What *is* this fixation on the perverse—the deviant, the macabre, the diseased?

Jack B. Haskins, late professor of journalism at the University of Tennessee, offered this definition of morbid curiosity: "an enduring unusually strong attraction to information about highly unpleasant events and objects that are irrelevant to the individual's life."

My own experience tells me that Haskins is wrong. My attraction to the macabre might well be directed toward "unpleasant events," but it's certainly not irrelevant. My Gothic sensibilities, though sometimes silly, to be sure (what man over forty monthly watches Freund's *The Mummy*?), have inspired my writing and fueled my intellect. Morbidity seems essential to others as well, and maybe not just to humans.

Consider a scene. On the edge of the savanna, an elephant rots. The cow had been sick for a week, stumbling, alone, over the hot plain. Ten days ago, it fell in the dust and died. Now its flesh has decomposed. Only the large skeleton recalls the mammoth's grandeur.

A herd lurches near to the bones. The pack is composed of females, all related, led by the matriarch. They've had no prior contact with the dead beast.

They stand over the corpse. With their trunks, they gently probe the bones, seizing choice remains, turning them in the sun, then dropping them. Eventually, each picks up a bone or tusk and carries it hundreds of yards away.

This behavior is difficult to account for. Other instances of animals attending to their dead seem to possess evolutionary value, to preserve shared genes. In many cases, the living linger near their fallen companions in hopes that breath remains and that they might be able to assist in the recovery. Elephants prop up collapsed members of their herds, ostensibly to keep them from suffocating. Dolphins aid their wounded by carrying them to the ocean's surface to take in air.

But what of the elephants who are simply fascinated by another rotting elephant, one obviously dead and not in the same herd? Is this an example of animal morbid curiosity? If so, what are the motivations for such behavior?

I haven't been able to find answers to these questions. Some scientists suggest that the elephants' practice bears evolutionary value. Studying the dead might give the living hints about how the creature died and so reveal behavior that should be avoided. Others, though, believe that the conduct of the elephants is not adaptive at all but simply an instance of normal instincts breaking down in the face of incomprehensible death.

I'd love to know if our being drawn to things dying or dead is an expression of a deep instinct that we share with certain animals, a drive for survival. Then our dark curiosities wouldn't be irrelevant, aberrant, or sinful but instead natural, useful.

The morbid is ameliorative: I really hope this is true, because I did something extremely strange at my grandmother's funeral.

8.

My father's parents lived in the Blue Ridge Mountains. In their drafty clapboard house, heated only by a cast-iron woodstove, they had learned that silence was almost the only solace in their impoverished, death-omened existence, through which roamed alcoholic brothers and daughters, preachers addled by superstition, and stained, unshaven men no one knew. Both were in their eighties by the time I was a boy, though they might have been two hundred, they were so hunched and calloused, wrinkled and resigned.

When we visited their house, set back from a one-lane dirt road, the men, great-uncles and uncles and cousins and in-laws, crowded into the living room and smoked and, like my grandparents, spoke little, and when they did it was of God or sickness or football. On clear days, they'd go outside and shoot green soda bottles with 12-gauge shotguns or listen to the cousin who brought his banjo play "I'll Fly Away." The women stood in the greasy, dark kitchen and watched my grandmother fry chicken.

I never liked the visits to this house in the holler. Enamored of our clean, modern ranch house in a bright leafy suburb sixty miles away, and also of the latest technology (such as Atari or handheld computer football), I frowned on what I saw as back-country squalor.

But it was more than that. I had genuine fear. The primitive house of my grandparents threatened my youthful persona, made of brand names and the quest for hipness. With its archaic woodsmoke, the dwelling summoned me to leave my thin hobbies and get into visceral mountain matters: hunting, deer meat, hounds, rusty pickups, Camel cigarettes, flannel, tent revivals, Bibles well thumbed, faith hard as flint, the Devil.

For the past ten years, I've been addicted to the music gathered by Harry Smith in his 1952 *Anthology of American Folk Music*, a disquieting dream from the mountains of Appalachia, through which Doc Boggs, Clarence Ashley, Furry Lewis, the Carter Family, and Blind Lemon Jefferson wail their weird mixtures of winter dirge and gallows humor. The music critic Greil Marcus describes what it's like to listen: you are "cast into a charnel house that bears a disturbing resemblance to everyday life: to wishes and fears, difficulties and satisfactions that are, as you know, as plain as day, but also, in the voices of those who are now singing, the work of demons—demons like your neighbors, your family, your lovers, yourself." I don't know if I believe in direct genetic inheritance, but I suspect that this music speaks to me so profoundly because my very DNA recalls the haunted souls of my Blue Ridge ancestors.

There is another, more disturbing event that convinces me of my Appalachian birthright. When I was in graduate school in New York City, I got a call from my dad. My grandmother had died the night before, and he wanted me to come down for the funeral.

The next day I found myself in a weary funeral home. Black dust covered the low-hung ceiling and the crimson carpet hadn't been cleaned in years. I sat with the other mourners in metal folding chairs. Before us was the minister, and behind him, elevated on a small stage, the open coffin. I had never seen a real corpse before.

The last time I had visited my grandmother, about a year earlier, she had looked terrible, almost bent double. Unable to raise her head to look at me, she tilted her rheumy eyes upward and held out her hand. Arthritis had contorted it into a claw. She smelled of earth and wintergreen snuff.

Sweating in the overheated funeral home, waiting for the minister to stop, I decided that I didn't want to see my grandmother dead. I would walk quickly from the building after the benediction.

But I didn't. I veered to the corner of the room and loitered alone, while my relatives paid their respects. When the crowd cleared, I stole up to the coffin. I stared at the face, its rigid closed eyes, and glancing around, I held my index finger only inches from her dead hand. But before I could touch it, I heard approaching voices and exited out a side door.

9.

Colin Beer of Rutgers University, a psychologist, wouldn't call my episode randomly spooky, a visit from the perverse imp. He would say that I was expressing an instinct that I share not with animals but with humans alone. In his words, nothing in the animal kingdom, not even the "necromantic behavior of elephants," "quite adds up to human morbid curiosity in either content or intensity of preoccupation"—nothing, he continues, "to match the public torturing of condemned prisoners such as Byron wrote about in one of his letters, or the horrors that fill the annals of witchcraft, or the preoccupation with sacrifice, suffering, and martyrdom that looms so large in the history of religion."

For Beer, morbid curiosity might be a "by-product" of imagination, which probably evolved along with intellect and language in response to environmental or social pressures that required more sophisticated communication techniques. A group's ability to share information about nearby dangers or hunting opportunities, for instance, gave its members a major adaptive advantage, enabling them to weather potentially harmful changes by exploring new modes of survival.

If Beer is right, then, our morbid fixations are connected to an essential component of language and imagination alike: the ability to relate to others in ways beneficial to a group. The trait most useful for forging these human relationships is empathy, the capacity to identify with the pleasures and pains of another. Our attraction to the macabre is on some level a desire to experience someone else's suffering.

This idea comforts me. It tells me that my macabre fascinations are expressions of a deep human need to feel another's pain and also useful for the survival of species and individual.

We thought that the sunshine only—with its green elms and violets—was the object most worthy of our attention. Now the nighttime and all those cemeteries replace the day as the country most alive. Now the itch to touch a corpse is normal, noble.

10.

But these claims might well be only speculation, and, in my case, more than that: wishful thoughts from someone who's read too much Poe and is prone, rather immaturely, to romanticize death. Certainly other scientists would probably say so. Some claim that morbid curiosity is only a desire for strong physiological arousal: the unseemly attracts us because it is more stimulating to our bodies than are more pleasant events. This theory implies that repeated exposure to the morbid can desensitize us and thus result in an appetite for increasingly horrific episodes. For instance, as television viewers require more and more destruction to achieve their desired physiological stimulation, they will become less and less capable of empathizing with actual suffering. Morbid events will devolve into commodities—objects to be consumed for crass pleasure. The result of this cultural insensitivity will be, in the words of Jack B. Haskins (whom I cited above), "an increase in anxieties, pessimism, distrust in other people and institutions, and non-caring which will have negative survival value for our species."

Well, if fascination with the macabre is unethical, then I'm one heinous bastard. See you in hell. I won't be alone when I greet you. My nine-year-old daughter, Una, will be right by my side.

Several months ago, Una asked me to read her a story that would give her nightmares. When I asked why, she said that she enjoyed bad dreams; they were like movies, and they didn't really scare her. In particular, her nightmares reminded her of the old horror films she and I used to watch Wednesday nights. *The Mummy, Frankenstein, Dracula, The Wolf Man*: these classic Universal films never frightened her, nor did other dark stories, such as the early Batman comics. She in fact loved monsters of all kinds, and spent many afternoons drawing them, mainly deranged robots and the folkloric Japanese demons known as the wicked *oni*.

I admit that my daughter, though by most standards normal, is a little unique in her love of monsters. But her attraction to the macabre puts her firmly in the mainstream. Her playmates and classmates, boys and girls alike, constantly turn sticks into weapons, squash insects, concoct bloody fantasies, and pretend to kill each other.

Children have probably always been drawn to violence. Certainly the centuries-long popularity of gruesome fairy tales suggests that this is so. In the nineteenth century, European scholars anthologized some of these stories. The most famous of these collections is that of the Brothers Grimm. Their stories—including "Cinderella," "Hansel and Gretel," "Little Red Cap," and "Sleeping Beauty"—originated long before, probably in the Middle Ages, when the tales were a thriving part of a popular culture at odds with ecclesiastical authorities. The narratives were frequently bawdy, violent burlesques providing relief from oppressive rules. When the Grimms expurgated these stories for polite audiences, they removed the erotic elements, more or less, but kept the violence, and thus presented "a world in which villains are regularly decapitated or boiled in oils and giants are slain or tricked into cutting the throats of their children."

Those are the words of Maria Tatar, a professor of German at Harvard. She argues that the violence was likely retained to teach kids a lesson. Take another famous German children's book from the nineteenth century, Heinrich Hoffmann's *Der Struwwelpeter*, translated as *Shaggy Peter*, from 1845. In one story, Conrad the Thumb-sucker is chased by a sinister-looking tailor who carries a huge pair of shears. When the tailor catches the boy, he lops off both thumbs. Another tale features Pauline, who likes to play with matches. She accidentally burns herself to death, and her story grimly concludes with two of her friends mourning at her grave. Then there's little Kaspar. He won't eat his soup, and so dwindles to a stick figure, and ends up, like Pauline, dead. A soup bowl serves as his tombstone.

Parents might believe that this hyperbolic violence keeps children in line, but the strategy frequently backfires, with children expressing unbridled merriment at the macabre episodes they are supposed to fear. More recent authors of children's books—Lewis Carroll, Roald Dahl, and Maurice Sendak—have tried to sympathize with this juvenile delight. Recall the scene in Dahl's *Charlie and the Chocolate Factory* in which the gluttonous Augustus Gloop suffers the gruesome grindings of the fudge machine.

Tatar says that what distinguishes children from adults is precisely what sadistic moral tales have tried to repress: "exuberance, energy, mobility, irrepressibility, irreverence, curiosity, audacity." Among these powers—constant challenges to the "civilizing" agendas of adults—curiosity seems the most important because it "fuels development" by driving children to "push the limits of what is permitted to them and to ignore prohibitions." Time to blow up Barbie.

Ken, too. At least Great Shape Ken. In addition to encouraging cognitive growth, violent fantasies help children "to feel stronger, to access their emotions, to take control of their anxieties, to calm themselves down in the face of real violence, to fight their way through emotional challenges and lift themselves to new developmental levels."

So claims Gerard Jones. In *Killing Monsters: Why Children Need Fantasy, Super Heroes, and Make-Believe Violence,* Jones argues that young people identify with fictional violence because it makes them feel *powerful* in a "scary, uncontrollable world." Children's fascination with havoc has less to do with action and more to do with how the action makes them feel. Children like to feel strong. Those committing violence are strong. By pretending to be these violent figures, children take on their strength to negotiate daily dangers.

According to Jones, fallacious logic keeps many adults from accepting this claim. Many grown-ups believe that violent media cause violent deeds. But these adults would never apply this reasoning to other kinds of media. Who would say that game shows lead to greed or that representations of charity create a more generous world?

Research on children is troublesome, too, mainly because the relationships of children to morbid fantasies are simply too complex to be understood by empirical data alone. For example, though some fieldwork ostensibly supports the causal argument—violent fictions cause aggressive actions—other experiments contradict the theory. One study showed that boys from well-to-do households aren't really affected by violent videos at all and that male child delinquents actually become *less* aggressive after witnessing media violence.

For Jones, the emotional lives of children are likely to remain intractable to a scientific model of research because a "child's imagination doesn't behave like the cells of the body, with a predictable, somatic response."

Jones's arguments support what Maurice Sendak, master of children's macabre, thought all along: in empowering children to navigate effectively a sinister environment, violent stories indeed make young ones less instead of more destructive.

Putting the theory into practice, Sendak got in trouble. Though it's now valued as a classic, when *Where the Wild Things Are* came out in 1963, many criticized it for being too scary for kids. A cantankerous boy threatening to eat his mother; the mother sending him to bed without supper; surreal monsters— amalgams of chickens, rams, hogs, dogs—on a dusky island: these factors troubled reviewers and offended librarians. The book was banned in some districts.

As the response to the 2008 film version of the book shows, some still believe that the story is too frightening for youngsters. Sendak doesn't care. When asked what he'd say to parents criticizing the movie, he answered: "I would tell them to go to hell. That's a question I will not tolerate." If children can't handle the darker elements of the movie, they can, Sendak continues, "go home," or "wet [their] pants." Life is scary, Sendak emphasizes, so why shouldn't children's stories reflect this fact? He praises particular European films, such as François Truffaut's *The 400 Blows* or Lasse Hallström's *My Life as a Dog*, for their authentic renderings of childhood fear. In contrast, he asserts, most kid movies in America are "squeamish" before reality. Sendak places himself firmly in the European tradition when he says that the writer's "trick" is to turn suffering "into art."

With his own troubled past, Sendak did exactly that. He was born into a poor Brooklyn household a few years before the Great Depression. While jostled from apartment to apartment—since his mother hated the smell of fresh paint, the family moved every time a landlord decided to brighten up the walls—he endured measles, double pneumonia, and scarlet fever. His itinerant life and frequent sickness—not to mention his stuttering and weight problem—made it hard for him to find playmates. He spent much of his time in bed, reading comics or drawing. He also listened to unnerving stories about his parents' harrowing past. For instance, his mother, a Polish Jew, told of hiding in the basement while Cossacks ravaged her village. World War II brought further affliction to Sendak. His Polish aunts and uncles died in the Holocaust, and his sister's fiancé was killed in combat.

Sendak's morbid imagination helped him endure these troubles. His art saved him from the truth. He said as much in his 1964 acceptance speech for his Caldecott—a prestigious children's book award. No doubt recalling his difficult childhood, he claimed that "[w]hat is too often overlooked is the fact that from their earliest years children live on familiar terms with disrupting emotions . . . fear and anxiety are an intrinsic part of their everyday lives . . . they continually cope with frustration as best they can. And it is through fantasy that children achieve catharsis. It is the best means they have for taming Wild Things."

This idea goes back to Aristotle: fictions about destructive emotions can purge these feelings. An aesthetic experience of the macabre—in pictures, books, films, maybe even video games—is useful, therapeutic. The child loves violent fantasies as she would a wizened mentor, a skilled guide. We, as adults, can learn from this: the morbid builds morale.

I'm not a depraved parent after all. Una can draw demons (she prefers them in powder blue) with impunity, and later gleefully read about James's giant peach squashing Spiker and Sponge. Too early, though, for the gore of Jason and Freddie. When to take your little one to Elm Street?

12.

A throng of spectators waits silently in a dark room. They sit in rows and stare straight ahead. Clicking breaks the quiet. A yellow beam thrusts into the gloom. The men and women, now in shadows and nervously murmuring, gaze at the light's target: a sixteen-by-twelve sheet of white paper hanging on the wall toward which they face.

On the blankness appears a grayish blur. The phantasm clarifies, and words emerge: "The Great Train Robbery." Then, blended in gray and black and white, a man sits at a desk. The image moves, as though alive.

The audience gasps. They've never seen anything like this. When two cowboys rush in and point pistols at the man, the crowd convulses again and braces—the figures might leap out of the screen. What's real and what's illusion?

Successive scenes exacerbate the disquiet. The bandits force the man, a railroad telegraph operator, to order an oncoming train to stop, and then knock him unconscious. The thieves murder the train's messenger. They beat another man down and toss him from the speeding train. They kill a passenger trying to escape. They gun down their pursuers before they meet their own bloody demise.

The spectators clench, duck, shut their eyes, reopen them quickly—they can't miss the carnage. They are mesmerized by the savagery.

The last murderer dies, and everyone relaxes. It's over. But on the screen is the living face of one of the robbers. He aims his pistol at the crowd and shoots. Everyone screams, dives to the floor. Seconds pass, and then, when the audience members realize they're not dead, they let out a collective laugh and yell for the film to run again.

This happened in December 1903, during the New York premiere of the first narrative film, Edwin S. Porter's cinematic rendition of a robbery that actually took place in Wyoming. In a week, *The Great Train Robbery* was running in eleven theaters in or near the city. Soon the movie was playing throughout America, eventually earning $2 million, an immense sum at the time. Repeatedly, the American public fell into rapture over the bloodshed. They hit the deck at the story's end and begged for more.

The film's producer, Thomas Edison, wanted this reaction. As he wrote of the movie in his company's catalogue, his film's subject was "sensational and highly tragic" and thus sure to "make a decided 'hit' whenever shown." With uncanny perception, Edison realized at the beginning of the age of narrative cinema that audiences love looking at terrible things. The inventor knew, and capitalized on, what film directors have exploited ever since: violence pulls, and is as likely to inspire ecstasy as terror.

13.

We've all been on that floor—debased and exhilarated by our fears, scared to death but more alive than ever. Part of it is the rush—the same exhilaration we get from roller coasters or white-water rafting. But there's more, I think, and it's psychological—something inside of us, deep and dark, is actually up there on that screen, doing the killing or being killed. The screen is a magical mirror revealing portions of our psyches that we try to hide from ourselves and the world, those sadistic and masochistic urges: I want to whack my boss; I deserve to be punished. But even if we say that we are ashamed of our internal aggressor and victim, our narcissism prevails: I can't help but gaze lovingly at that cinematic glass, even though I'm ugly as sin. "Beauty is only skin deep, but ugly goes clean to the bone." So Dorothy Parker. Our worst self is more captivating than anyone else's brighter being.

Carl Jung, who founded, along with Freud, psychoanalysis, believed that we like to witness violence precisely because it, the watching, allows us to entertain our most destructive impulses without actually harming ourselves or others. Jung himself was drawn to darkness. When he was four, he couldn't stop thinking about the corpse of another four-year-old boy, who had drowned in a nearby river. Around the time the child was found, Jung almost leapt into the same deadly rapids; he was saved only by the swift grip of the maid. To this suicidal urge, the adolescent Jung added a fixation on ghosts, nightly encountering haunts throughout his house.

Jung continued this "corpse preoccupation," as he called it, his entire life, and it informed one of his most lasting contributions to our understanding of the human psyche: the idea of the shadow. He believed that the self is composed of three levels—the conscious ego, the personal unconscious, and the collective unconscious. The personal unconscious is made of repressed memories and instincts unique to an individual's history. The collective unconscious, in contrast, transcends the particular. It is a ubiquitous, timeless reservoir of archetypes that organize conscious existence. One of these archetypes is the shadow, an archive of all that we hate about ourselves, usually morbid impulses, such as the propensity toward melancholy or suicidal and murderous urges. The shadow's favored forms are devils, demons, imps, vampires, werewolves, goblins, enemies of planet and country and town, and other people who just irritate the hell out of us.

Because we loathe the shadow, we push it deep into the unconscious, hoping to forget about it, make it go away. But it won't. The harder we repress it, the more aggressively it rebels. Think of water pressure in a hose: the longer we impede its flow, the more its force builds, until it explodes, a geyser. A repressed shadow floods our minds with harmful visions. It bedevils us with traumatic nightmares that can make our days neurotic.

Or, worse, it foments outright psychosis, tempting us into projecting our own internal demons onto others, usually loved ones. We distort our parents or wives or children or friends into monsters and so sabotage our most valuable relationships.

Though we hate the shadow, we also secretly desire it, because in our deepest recesses we actually yearn for ruin. We might profess pristine piety, but we really have sympathy for the devil. This is an obvious point—that we all have a dark side, a perverse imp. However, most of us deny it, trying to convince ourselves, and others, that our intentions are always righteous, our thoughts preeminently pure. And so we set up a game that seems silly, though in fact it's dead serious: don't let the right hand, bearing the torch of righteousness, know what the left hand, the sinister appendage, is doing. Such self-delusion ensures that we will remain divided against ourselves—reason versus the shadow, light against darkness—and moreover that the more nefarious side, because repressed to a place beyond awareness, will persist, unchecked, in its sowing of discord.

Jung thinks that mental health arises from concord between the darkness and the light. As long as we continue to demonize our morbid tendencies, we are only half a person, unnatural, out of whack, like day with no night, up without down. We become whole, healthy, harmonized, only when we acknowledge our innate addiction to the macabre. We must welcome it into our consciousness and embrace it. Then, almost as if by miracle, what earlier seemed simple destruction becomes necessary to life. No longer feared, demons turn angels. Luke offers his affection to Vader, and off comes the scary mask and there stands a father, loving and in need of love.

This reconciliation, like all negotiations between sworn

enemies, is extremely difficult to achieve, often requiring a lifetime of psychotherapy or disciplined meditation. How best to go about this work of welcoming the macabre, finding the light in the darkness, the darkness in the light? Through a Jungian teaching known as "active imagination."

As with his theory of the shadow, Jung's own life inspired his vision of therapeutic imagination. In 1913, Jung was suffering extreme melancholia over a conflict with Freud as well as severe doubts over the direction of his career. Exhausted, almost hopeless of recovering equilibrium, he decided one day, while sitting at his desk, just to give up. He would stop fighting his increasing despair; he would let the gloom consume him, come what may.

What happened next wasn't what he expected at all. Instead of simply going numb or blank, he fell into a reverie. He felt as though the ground were opening under his feet, and then he had the sensation of plunging into "the dark depths." As this fantasy continued, Jung realized that he was not falling into a meaningless void but instead into a plenitude of untapped energy, pure potential. Vitality flooded his being, for the first time in months.

Jung later interpreted this trance as an explanation of his despair and a call to hope. The fantasy was telling him, he believed, that his depression was a result of his overemphasis on his conscious ego—his desire to construct a clear, powerful, autonomous identity that would elevate him above Freud and forge a path to future success. But in holding too hard to the ego, out of fear of failure and a desire to prevail, Jung had neglected his unconscious, including his shadow, to the point where he was now alienated from an integral part of his own psyche. Hence his mental sickness—he was not whole. To recover health, his reverie advised, he needed to loosen his grip on his ego, delve into his unconscious, and there discover the powers he had been repressing. If he could understand the nature of these potencies, he could then find ways to connect them to his ego and thus restore harmony.

How to express the energies of the darkness and reconcile them to the light? Jung concluded that he must actively imagine words or pictures or structures that would accurately represent his unconscious and bring its energies fully into his conscious understanding. He first attempted this by filling notebooks with allegorical drawings and surreal parables. Later, he tried to capture and catalyze his hidden forces through architecture. He constructed a tower on Lake Zurich and periodically expanded it in width and height as he aged. He believed that the multifaceted edifice was a symbol of his self as it developed toward integration.

Jung's example suggests this bold idea: to create or to contemplate morbid phenomena is necessary for mental health, for expressing the psyche's destructive powers and reconciling them with bright reason. In going to the multiplex to check out the latest gore, I'm really plopping down on the therapist's couch, in quest of a more concordant and capacious and generous self. *Halloween* is the seventh heaven. The chain saw massacre: a kind of mass.

14.

The Great Train Robbery roused a cinematic ache that has increased each year in intensity. Our cultural desire for savage action films as well as for their near sibling, slasher horror movies, is by now insatiable. Even as we still struggle under the guilt of the torture in Abu Ghraib and Guantánamo Bay, even as we continue to fear terrorist attacks and mass shootings— even as all this brutality infects us—gruesome films like *Hostel*, *Saw*, *The Dark Knight*, and *300* are pervasive and extremely popular, attracting millions of viewers.

What is the perpetual draw of the horror film, a genre that, like a vampire, will not die? It flourishes in times of peace and war (more in times of war), powerful regardless of form— whether the Old Horror of James Whale's exotic creepy castles; the New Horror of John Carpenter and Tobe Hopper, where crazed killers lurk in the suburbs or backwoods; or the ironic horror of the *Scream* series.

Pauline Kael, though never a fan of the genre, claimed that scary movies infect us with the "fear sickness," that "crazy, inexplicable delight that children get out of terrifying stories that give them bad dreams." As Jason Zinoman explains in his recent book on horror, this exhilaration arises from the confusion of confronting "the forbidden, the taboo, and a hint of the disreputable." Such ecstatic bewilderment, he observes, recalls "the innocence of childhood." The gore of the R rating returns us to the joy of the G.

Surely this is one of the enduring enticements of cinematic creepiness. But there are perhaps other more complicated and serious attractions as well. Consider the recent defense of the genre mounted by the Mexican director Guillermo del Toro, maker of lyrical horror films such as *The Devil's Backbone* and *Pan's Labyrinth*. Sounding a little like Jung, he says, "Art is a reconstruction of the world, and violence and horror are absolutely as much part of the world as butterflies and happy faces. There are so many more people trying to sell us the bullshit that the world has to be happy and the world has to be sunny, and you have to have good breath and shiny hair. With this, we lose touch with imperfection and that makes for a really harsh, cold measure to live by. I think horror makes us human, because it reminds us of our imperfection."

This sentiment ennobles the genre, suggesting that it cuts through our vain delusions about what is real. Morris Dickstein, an English professor at the Graduate Center of the City University of New York, also believes in the value of horror films, which are, he claims, "a safe, routinized way of playing with death, like going to a roller coaster or parachute jump at an amusement park." Imagining our own end, we meditate on what we need to enliven our remaining years—what we shouldn't take for granted and what we should ignore.

For Will H. Rockett, another professor in the humanities,

horror films force us to face our own guilt over our own evil behaviors, so that we "might expiate real or imagined sins through
the controlled trauma of the film experience." This purgation
comes from our desire to transcend our isolation.

Aristotle developed a notion of purgation, too (invoked, as
we saw earlier, by Sendak in his justification of his book on wild
things). In his *Poetics*, Aristotle focuses on the literary genre of
tragedy, which he defines as "an imitation of an action that is
serious, complete, and of a certain magnitude." The tragic drama
features a hero of high social stature who, though noble, possesses a flaw that leads to his downfall, more catastrophic than
he deserves. Audiences experience pity and fear as they watch
the decline of the hero—pity over his suffering and fear of his
transgression.

These intense feelings, Aristotle claims, effect "the proper
purgation of these emotions." How this purgation—the translation of the Greek *katharsis*—actually works is not entirely clear,
but the gist is this: Expressing pity and fear in an artificial
setting, we drain these emotions from our systems and subse-
quently feel purified, relieved, refreshed.

Our desire for catharsis might explain why we like Hollywood tearjerkers in which wives or girlfriends or daughters
die—*Love Story, Terms of Endearment, Steel Magnolias*, and the like.
Catharsis might also account for our attraction to more oper-
atic fare, in which not one, but both lovers die: think of Tristan
and Isolde, Romeo and Juliet. (Indeed, many believe, with Wagner as their support, that romance reaches its zenith when the
lovers, preferably young and beautiful, die in each other's arms:
amour consummated for all eternity.) And, certainly, Aristotle's
theory can clarify the popularity of horror films: we are drawn

to gore because our vicarious experience of violence cleanses our hearts of aggression.

Aristotle is gospel for the great makers of the macabre. Stephen King claims that we "make up horrors to help us cope with the real ones," and the mode of coping is catharsis: horror stories, in film or fiction, are the "barber's leeches of the psyche, drawing not bad blood but anxiety." Hitchcock concurs: "Seeing a murder on television can be good therapy. It can help work off one's antagonism."

15.

Many challenge the catharsis theory, and not for the same reason Kael does (it's confusion, not purgation, that draws us to horror). A popular argument against the idea goes like this: Watching violence doesn't cleanse us of destructive impulses at all, but actually exacerbates them. Certain reformers, usually right-leaning espousers of "family values," are of course in love with this notion, since it justifies their projects to clean up our smut-filled and violence-ridden society (going to hell in a handbasket) through censorship laws.

Some studies have shown that violence in media does indeed cause aggression in "real life." But the evidence, as we saw in the earlier discussion of Gerard Jones, is far from conclusive. Meanwhile, regardless of scientific data, many humanists and artists continue to take Aristotle seriously, maintaining that the catharsis theory convincingly explains how we experience violent media and why macabre spectacles are valuable.

I put myself in this last category, and not because I'm a fan of Aristotle (really more of a Platonist), and not because I want to close ranks with my fellow humanists (English professors are some of the most tedious people on earth), and not because I've never really met a social scientist that I liked (I'm sure the problem's with me), and not because (am I lying to myself?) I need to ennoble what I like to do anyway: watch horror films.

I'm a defender of the catharsis theory, at least partially, and probably more than I'd like to admit, because I hate Tipper Gore. Not necessarily Tipper in her current form—troubled, I imagine (but maybe relieved), by her separation from Al—but the Tipper of 1985, when she went before Congress to lobby for warning labels on records containing lyrics that might be inappropriate for children.

Though I was only a freshman in college and woefully underinformed about current events, much less free-speech-versus-censorship debates, I took an interest in the hearings because I was obsessed with loathing poor Tipper. Fresh from resigning from West Point in protest of all things self-righteous, and otherwise in a general funk of sullen rebellion against my goody-goody Southern Baptist upbringing, I saw in Tipper everything I hated about the world just then: upright living, positive thinking, the G rating, and sentimentality, not to mention big hair. I also happened to be a fan of her opponents in the debate. First, Twisted Sister's front man, Dee Snider, with his crazed waist-length blond coif and loud French-whore makeup and deeply guttural passion for not taking shit from anybody. Next, Frank Zappa. I didn't know his music well but I liked his two children, Dweezil and Moon Unit, mainly for their names, and I liked that Frank said to Tipper, "May your shit come to life and kiss you on the face."

Watching those hearings on afternoons when I should have been reading Aristotle, I felt a visceral aversion to anything even approaching censorship. I realize that this was a simpleminded view—some things, of course, need censoring, such as child pornography—but it expressed a sensibility I still retain, and that I can now articulate more clearly: rarely, in the human world, can we establish clear causality.

This conviction—and not Tipper, truth be told—is the real reason that I can't join those scientists who dismiss catharsis and condemn violence in the media. I emphatically agree with Jones, who reminds us that a plethora of factors, some unknown and some graspable, generate any given human event—such as a nine-year-old saying "fuck" or a high school boy, hopped up on *Hostel* and *Saw*, committing a violent crime. To try to reduce these or any other societal phenomena to a particular cause— profane lyrics on a rap album or a horror film's gore—is to ignore the world's complexities, nuances, and contradictions. It's also, this reductive thinking, a kind of puritanism, whether it's applied to profanity, sex, or violence, since puritanical logic, in a general sense, is the narrow-minded attribution of evil to a set number of causes a little too well defined.

And so, now, twenty-five years after Tipper the good mother went head-to-head with Zappa, formerly of the Mothers of Invention, I continue to have a personal aversion toward people—be they social scientists or ministers or strict parents or conservative pundits—who claim that cinematic violence is responsible for some of our culture's ills. And now I'm prone, of course, to lean the other way: morbid curiosity arises from heterogeneous and complicated factors, and is quite possibly of value to society, either as a catalyst for purgation of aggression or the incorporation of the shadow.

Say that this view is an example of my immaturity, that

I'm letting teen petulance inform adult views. Say that I'm narrow-minded in my unwillingness to engage the sophisticated research of social scientists. Call me perversely contrarian, someone who needs to counter mainstream sentiment in order to get attention. Say whatever you want: I'll stick with Hitch and Stephen King and claim that violence in cinema isn't such a bad thing and might well be good for you. (Though I must admit that I'm a bit uncomfortable finding myself on the side of Dee Snider again; he's traded heavy metal for the horror film, writing and starring in the 1998 release *Strangeland*, about a sadist named Captain Howdy [Snider's character] who kidnaps teens and subjects them to gruesome body modification rituals.)

16.

It's really not all about my aversions, of course. I'm drawn to the catharsis theory—as well as the notion of the shadow—because both ideas have helped me explain how my fascination with the macabre has made my life fuller and richer.

If it's not clear by now, I'm a serious horror film fan, though I haven't seen *Strangeland* and probably won't. I'm especially in love with the artier ones, like *Night of the Living Dead*, *Rosemary's Baby*, *The Texas Chain Saw Massacre* (the original), Kubrick's *The Shining*, the first *Alien* film. I'm also an addict of the cinema's early efforts at terror: *Nosferatu*, *The Cabinet of Dr. Caligari*, *Frankenstein*, *The Mummy*, *The Bride of Frankenstein*. And more recent literate fare draws me as well: *Seven*, *Twenty-Eight Days*, Gerbinski's *The Ring*, *Pan's Labyrinth*, *Let the Right One In*. I also adore Hitchcock's dark psychodramas and I admit a penchant for more straightforward scariness—Carpenter's first *Halloween*, Craven's initial *Nightmare on Elm Street*, even *Scream* and *I Know What You Did Last Summer*.

One common thread among these—a strand shared with action films, violent television, and video games—is almost so obvious that we forget it: each relies on the storytelling techniques that separate fiction from nonfiction. Real life is mostly jumbled, confusing, and unpredictable. Fictional narratives often counteract the chaos with clear causal connections, reassuring rhythms of rising and falling action, characters who are complex yet consistent, revelations coming at just the right time, parts conforming to a harmonious whole, and conclusions that unify seemingly disparate events. These stories are *meaningful*: they push toward a discernible end and offer coherent messages.

In his *Philosophy of Horror*, Noël Carroll has argued that one of the primary attractions of scary movies is cognitive satisfaction. For Carroll, horror movies don't draw us so much for physical or emotional stimulation as for the pleasures of their plots, which explore problems—such as how to understand a monster and how to contain it—in riveting, suspenseful narratives that conclude with all questions answered. Take the Dracula story. The vampire fascinates us. We marvel at his supernatural powers, but also fear them. As the tale unfolds, his mysterious abilities are examined, explained, and eventually neutralized. We love this rhythm of problem and solution.

We miss this cadence when we witness violent images devoid of narrative finesse. Imagine an amateur videotape of a dinner party. Several people, maybe twelve, sit around a large table. In the center is a living monkey. With a hammer, one of the diners knocks the monkey unconscious. He splits open the skull, scoops out the still-beating brain, and serves it on a platter.

Switch scenes. There is a slaughterhouse. Bewildered, bellowing steers stagger through a chute. At the end of the line, a worker strikes each cow in the head with a sledgehammer.

Another man slices the throats. Still another hangs the bloody beeves from hooks.

Another sequence: a surgeon and his team surround a young girl prepared for an operation. The doctors sever the child's face from her skull and turn it inside out.

These are not images from a surreal Buñuel film, nor are they from *Faces of Death*, the 1978 mondo movie depicting actual dying. Instead, these crude, raw scenes were part of an experiment designed to determine reactions to seemingly real violence, and to understand how these differ from responses to obviously fake Hollywood mayhem.

In the study, male and female college students were shown the three films described above—none of which, I should add, was enhanced by sound effects, such as a musical score. Each student had the power to shut off the video whenever he or she wished. Most quit watching about halfway through, expressing disgust with the gory scenes. In contrast, students found an excessively violent scene from *Friday the 13th, Part III*, fully scored, to be "involving, exciting, and not boring." When this same clip was shown without the audio enhancement, it was less riveting.

It appears that the trappings of Hollywood movies, especially sound tracks, can make a horrific experience grippingly dramatic. The psychology professor Clark McCauley, who conducted the experiment, accounts for this result by invoking a Sanskrit text, the *Natyasastra*, written around AD 200–300. This work explores the concept *rasa*, "aesthetic or imaginative experience." In discussing tragedy—which shares traits with horror—the *Natyasastra* claims that although we try to avoid actual sadness, we are attracted to aesthetic renderings of grief because they pull us away from our "preoccupations with ourselves" and open us to the suffering of others. We transcend narcissism and empathize.

This transcendence grows from catharsis: normally self-interested feelings, like pity and fear, are purified of their egotism and connected to more altruistic concerns, such as how to assuage the suffering of the collective. Fiction encourages this emotional free play. We are invited to explore without the pressure of consequences.

McCauley applies the *Natyasastra* to horror films. The fear and disgust inspired by such films invite us to sound the depths of our humanity, to contemplate the origins of our own disgusts and fears, or to put ourselves in the place of the characters in the story, killer and victim alike. In either case, if we could respond positively to the invitation, we might be expanded, awakened, enlightened—to a great and possibly transformative degree when we behold the more brilliant works of horror.

Of course, life is messy, as likely to be selfish and stupid as expansive and wise, and so it's the rare occasion that making or watching a film is devoid of egotism's blindness. Some scary movies will exploit suffering more than open us to its transforming depths. And most fans of the horror genre are probably going to be ignorant of their favorite films' invitations to transcend selfishness. Still, the potential is there: viewing a scary movie, especially one by a true artist—a del Toro or a Kubrick or a Polanski—can, however infrequently, call forth what is best in us and maybe make us a little more empathetic and charitable than we were before.

17.

In 1819, Francisco Goya bought a house called Quinta del Sordo (Country House of the Deaf Man), located on a lonely plot outside Madrid. The house was named thus because its former owner had, like Goya, lost his hearing. The Spanish artist was seventy-two when he retired here. After a long and vexed life, a chiaroscuro of public success and private insanity, he craved tranquillity.

He didn't find it. Soon after moving in, he began to paint nightmarish images on the interior walls—a father devouring a son, for example, and beastly witches convening, in a nocturnal forest, with a he-goat. These works, fifteen in all, distributed throughout the house, were called the Black Paintings.

The most disturbing of these images is the one devoted to filicide, later called, after Goya's death, *Saturn Devouring His Son*. The elderly Goya no doubt had Saturn much on his mind; this was the god and the planet associated with melancholia, a condition that had bedeviled the artist from middle age onward and had served as the gloomy muse for *Courtyard with Lunatics* (1794) and *The Sleep of Reason Produces Monsters* (1799). Now, as he approached death, with his chronic sorrow hardening into misanthropic cynicism, Goya pushed beyond the medieval and Renaissance picture of Saturn as brooding philosopher to the deity's first mythological guise: Cronus, paranoid and vicious.

The classical Greek pantheon began when Gaia, the earth goddess, and Uranus, the deity of the sky, produced the twelve Titans. Cronus was the youngest of this group, and also the leader. Envious of his father's power, he led a rebellion, and eventually castrated and killed Uranus with a sickle. The son took the father's place, and, for a time, ruled well.

Then Gaia told Cronus a prophecy: Just as he had murdered his father, so one of his children would destroy him. In hopes of avoiding this fate, Cronus decided to devour each of his children at the moment of its birth. Ops, his wife and sister, gave birth to gods and goddesses destined to Olympian greatness: Demeter, Hera, Hades, Hestia, and Poseidon. Cronus ate them all.

Tormented, Ops contrived to hide one child from her ravenous husband. She replaced this babe with a rock, which Cronus, fooled, consumed. This infant grew into Zeus, who overthrew his father, as the prophecy predicted, and made the old god vomit up his siblings. Zeus then imprisoned this vanquished king, along with the other Titans, in Tartarus.

In Goya's painting, you first see Cronus's eyes, slightly crossed. They are wide, wild, and fixed, as though this unearthly creature has for days been staring, fevered and entranced, into a blackness known only to him. His countenance is more beast than deity—muddy brown, like soiled fur, and haloed by an unkempt mane. But the face is mostly maw: strained to the point of ripping. Jammed into his mouth is the bloody arm of his small son's corpse, already decapitated and lacking a limb.

Compared with this ghoulish perversity, most Hollywood horror films are cartoonish (with notable exceptions, such as the artfully Gothic works listed above, especially *Pan's Labyrinth*, which actually bases its most terrifying monster, the eyeless white man, on Goya's painting). If we really saw an insane father gorging himself on his child, we would be traumatized for life. We are glad, though, to gaze at Goya's rendering. It hangs in one of the most distinguished museums in the world, the Prado in Madrid, to which tourists trek in droves to cherish this nightmare.

18.

In 1757, Edmund Burke, a philosopher, explained why we are drawn to terrible things, aesthetic or actual. In *A Philosophical Enquiry into the Origin of Our Ideas of the Sublime and Beautiful*, he develops a distinction that has become essential for theoreticians of horror—between the beautiful and the sublime. For Burke, beautiful experiences inspire pleasurable, affectionate feelings as well as serenity and languor. Such encounters involve objects that harmonize unity and diversity, such as leaves, garden slopes, streams, the feathers of exotic birds. The interplay between intricacy and uniformity is charming.

The sublime, on the other hand, is nerve-racking, turbulent. Obscure and confusing yet also stunning, irresistible, sublime events inspire horror and astonishment. A dense passage in Milton, for instance, or a cyclone or a god can hurry the "mind . . . out of itself" into bewildering complexity, dangerous but also powerful, sickening and exhilarating at once. This is the duplicity of the sublime: pain and pleasure, anxiety and minds expanding.

Burke was concerned with how the sublime affects the

senses. Immanuel Kant, Burke's near contemporary, studied the sublime's impact on the mind. According to Kant, the sublime experience occurs when vast energies or expanses overwhelm our sense-making mechanisms—our capacity to translate raw encounters into concepts or images. This failure causes discomfort, but also joy, for just when the understanding and the imagination falter, another faculty, the reason, intuits forces that transcend nature, such as infinity and eternity.

Essential for this mixture of fear and ecstasy is *distance*. This is Burke on witnessing horror: "It is certain, that it is absolutely necessary my life should be out of any imminent hazard, before I can take a delight in the sufferings of others, real or imaginary, or indeed in anything else from any cause whatsoever."

Kant agrees. From both philosophers, it follows: Though we must be out of harm's way to undergo a sublime experience, we can't be too far from the action; the closer, the better. We thrill to the threat of the dangers—deep down, knowing we're secure. Watching a public hanging, we are aware that we are safe from the gallows but there is nonetheless probably a small portion of us that thinks: This could happen to me. Stowed safely behind our double-paned bay windows, many of us enjoy storms; part of the attraction is the chance, extremely remote, of lightning striking the chimney.

When we are too far away from a sublime event, the tingle subsides; overly near, and the fright is too much. In the middle ground thrives the sublime, the morbid aesthetic. Here on this tumultuous border, we find fiction is no longer enough—those disaster flicks, movie monsters. We want real wildness—actual destruction, and flesh-and-blood criminals whose unbounded violence inspires our greater awe.

19

Ted Bundy: the good-looking law student from the Northwest who killed at least thirty-five young women, usually by bludgeoning and strangling them, sometimes committing rape beforehand or necrophilia afterward.

John Wayne Gacy: a successful Chicago businessman who played "Pogo the Clown" for block parties; he also tortured, raped, and murdered thirty-three young men and boys, burying the bodies of twenty-six of them in the crawl space beneath his home.

Jeffrey Dahmer: he murdered seventeen young boys and men, many of them of Asian or African descent; his methods involved torture, rape, dismemberment, necrophilia, and cannibalism. He often stored body parts in his freezer so he could eat them later.

There are others: David Berkowitz, the Son of Sam, who killed six women to appease a demon dwelling in his neighbor's dog; Ed Gein, the murderer and grave robber who made clothes and furniture out of human skin (and who inspired Norman Bates of *Psycho* as well the Buffalo Bill character in *The Silence of the Lambs*). And so many more: the Zodiac Killer, Charles Stark-weather, Gary Leon Ridgeway, Hadden Clark, and Aileen Wuornos (one of the few women to murder serially).

These killers have committed some of the most disturbing crimes in history—transgressions that horrify and anger me and make me want to do things that go against my grain, like purchase a firearm or never let my child out of my sight or endorse capital punishment. I suspect you react in much the same way.

Why, then, this scene?

It's 1992, and the sixty-fourth annual Academy Awards ceremony is about to begin. The audience awaits the entrance of Billy Crystal, the evening's host. Two men dressed as medical orderlies roll onto the stage an upright gurney. A man is strapped to it. He wears a tuxedo, as one might expect at an awards show, but covering his face, from the eyes down, is what seems to be a brown mask with a small square opening at the mouth. It's not a mask. It's a muzzle. Then it comes clear. This is Crystal himself, playing the part of Hannibal Lecter, the brilliant psychiatrist and cannibalistic serial killer in *The Silence of the Lambs*, one of the year's most popular and acclaimed films. The audience explodes into laughter.

Gory murder becomes acceptable commodity. Not only was a psychopathic murderer the inspiration for the most famous Oscar opening of all time; he was also the most important figure in the academy's favorite film. *The Silence of the Lambs* won five awards, and not just any five. The big five: best actor (Anthony Hopkins, for his iconic performance of Lecter); best actress (Jodie Foster as Clarice, the protagonist); best director (Jonathan Demme); best adapted screenplay (Ted Tally); and best picture.

The movie has grossed almost $273 million since its release. Its critical reputation has flourished. It is number fifty-five on the American Film Institute's top-one-hundred list. Lecter is listed as the institute's top villain of all time. One of Lecter's jokes about his cannibalism—"A census taker once tried to test me. I ate his liver with some fava beans and a nice Chianti"— has made it to number twenty-one on the top-movie-quotes list.

By now the film and its infamous killer are pop cultural fixtures. Thomas Harris, author of the novel on which *The Silence of the Lambs* was based, has produced another Lecter-inspired fiction, *Hannibal*. Ridley Scott has turned this book into a film. Another director, Brett Ratner, filmed Harris's prequel to *Silence*, called *The Red Dragon*.

Silence has sparked an Off-Off-Broadway comedy, the 2005 *Silence! The Musical*. It has appeared, in moments of parody, in *The Family Guy*, *The Simpsons*, *South Park*, *Clerks 2*, *Gold Member: Austin Powers 2*, *The Office*, and even a children's show, *The Fairly Odd Parents*.

There's also currently a thriving Hannibal Lecter memorabilia market. One can purchase a replica of Lecter's muzzle, Lecter action figures, miniature models of Lecter, Lecter costumes, and Lecter T-shirts and posters.

20

Why is Lecter so lovable? Why is *Dexter*, the Showtime series about a serial killer with a mordant wit, so popular? How do we account for the huge sales of books on monstrous psychopaths, such as Anne Rule's *The Stranger Beside Me*, her account of Ted Bundy?

David Schmid addresses such questions in *Natural Born Celebrities: Serial Killers in American Culture*, hailed by Joyce Carol Oates as a "persuasively argued, meticulously researched, and compelling examination of the media phenomenon of the 'celebrity criminal' in American culture." Schmid is most interested in this paradox: although Americans roundly condemn serial killers as monsters, our culture still treats these murderers as if they were famous actors or musicians.

In our media markets, serial killers thrive. In the competition for high ratings, serious news outlets and tabloids alike must draw on the most attention-grabbing stories possible, and lurid murderers provide eye-catching copy.

There are also psychological reasons why repetitive murderers are celebrities. We are fascinated by these criminals because they break constraining laws and conventions and, in their place, establish their own rules of behavior. They do what they want, when they want, while we labor under the burden of "thou shalt not."

This duplicity is archetypally American. Think of our vexed cultural relationship to the cowboy. We might disapprove of his lawless gunslinging and Indian killing, but we laud his indifference to the East Coast status quo and his fearless trekking into the Western wilds.

The serial killer, Schmid asserts, is as American as apple pie, a revelation of the imperialistic aggression (we must destroy enemies of the American way) lurking underneath our self-righteous puritanism (we must construct godly cities). He is our true familiar, what we love about our American selves and hate, John Wayne and Ted Kaczynski at once. He is our Jungian shadow: symbol of all that we want to forget about ourselves but that nevertheless is essential to our being.

21.

Psycho as saint, murderer as oracle: strange as these phrases sound, they might be disturbingly accurate. What marks a holy man, a sacred woman? One token of apotheosis is the relic—an object whose alleged power seems to confirm the potency of the person with whom it is associated. Take the Shroud of Turin, the linen on which appears an image of what might be the face of the crucified Christ. Many Christians think this is the cloth in which Jesus' dead body was wrapped. In 2010, the shroud was made available for public viewing for the eighteenth time in its long history. More than two million visitors traveled to gaze.

The shroud is one of many such relics in the history of Christianity. The most prominent ones in circulation during the Middle Ages were bits of wood ostensibly from Christ's cross. There were also more grotesque artifacts: Jesus' foreskin, for instance, or the body parts, bones, or hair of saints, such as the elbow of St. Augustine.

The Catholic Church no longer allows the sale of relics, and few believers are interested in them. There is a rather large market for relics of another kind, though, no less fascinating: objects associated with serial killers.

"Sacred" comes from the Latin *sacer*, which means both holy and accursed. Saints, no matter how much they represent the values of a culture's religious system, are set apart from the main. They defy ordinary science and evoke great violence. Jesus, consummately saintly, is a freak, one could say, for being the only human, at least in the Christian tradition, who is also God. And what do Christians do to this aberrant creature? They heap upon him all of their loathsome acts and in so doing essentially turn him—according to a famous theory of the anthropologist René Girard—into a scapegoat, a mutant, shunned, tortured, and killed.

Jesus, despite his blessedness, is monstrous. Serial killers, accursed, turn holy. Though they rape and kill, these criminals also embody deep collective desires: to be beyond law, to make one's own law. And even if their acts of killing are perversely baroque, they are also strangely sublime, so extravagantly violent that they push the mind beyond concept and image to abysmal forces. The serial killer is a scapegoat, too, a creature onto whom we project all that we detest about ourselves: our violent fantasies, our unseemly dreams. Instead of hating ourselves, we abhor him.

22.

On May 31, 1986, Hadden Clark, a cross-dressing schizophrenic from Bethesda, Maryland, killed a six-year-old girl named Michele Dorr. He used a butcher knife. After he was caught by the police, he confessed to killing other girls and women. Once they were dead, he drank their blood.

Clark became a celebrity. Millions read Adrian Havill's biography of the killer, called *Born Evil*. Many of the same devoured Alec Wilkinson's feature on Clark in *The New Yorker*. Network and cable news shows provided detailed coverage of Clark, and entire programs—airing on the Biography Channel, the Crime and Investigation Network, and Court TV—were devoted to him.

Almost twenty-five years later, Clark is still in the spotlight, though a much dimmer one. He is serving a life sentence in a penitentiary in Montgomery County, Maryland, but he maintains his notoriety by selling objects made valuable by his contact with them—in other words, relics. He markets his wares through websites that traffic in murderer memorabilia, or "murderabilia." One such website, redrumautographs.com, was in the summer of 2010 offering a cartoonish picture of two little girls, drawn by Clark and authenticated by his hand- and footprints ($169.99); an empty granola cereal box whose contents were consumed by Clark ($49.99); an unopened granola bar Clark purchased at the prison store ($16.99); cough drops once in Clark's mouth, with a signed note ($19.99); a bar of soap used by Clark, also with a signed note ($19.99); a toothbrush used by Clark ($29.99); and a large number of other cartoonlike drawings of young girls (all going for $29.99).

Aside from the broker fees, Clark gets the proceeds, which he can spend or save as he sees fit. This feels wrong, especially when we think of the friends and relatives of Clark's victims. How must the mother of Michele Dorr feel when she learns that there are people out there so enthralled by her little girl's killer that they'll pay good money for his stale toothbrush? And what about when she hears that this brutal murderer is prospering from this money, that he can procure an extra box of cereal, maybe, or a special granola bar, or some smokes, either for his own enjoyment or to barter with other inmates?

Clark appears to harbor no remorse. A female reporter once wrote to ask him about murderabilia. In his response, Clark requested that she send him a Girl Scout calendar and also a picture of herself, when she was "a little girl in dresses." "I love girls," he added.

Dave Reichert, a Republican congressman from the state of Washington, has been at the forefront of a movement to shut down the selling of murderabilia. Before becoming a politician, Reichert was a detective, and he led the hunt for the so-called Green River Killer, who in the 1980s and '90s dumped the corpses of his forty-eight victims, all prostitutes, into the dark water. The authorities eventually caught this serial murderer—one Gary Ridgeway, a truck painter, now serving a life sentence—but not before fishing out the rotted cadavers. Reichert understandably remains shaken by his pursuit of Ridgeway, which forced him to stare for weeks at putrescent bodies and required him repeatedly to witness the inconsolable grief of the victims' families. Reichert says that his grim memories of these horrible days are *his* murderabilia—not the used cereal boxes and childish art of a heinous murderer.

Despite the efforts of Reichert and others, the murderabilia trade continues to thrive. There are simply too many loopholes in the current laws prohibiting prisoners from profiting from their crimes.

A self-portrait by Gacy can go as high as $1,995; a handwritten note by Dahmer, $1,700.

Is there something hypocritical about decrying the sale of murderabilia? David Schmid believes so. He thinks it's "pretty rich for a nation that regards Truman Capote's *In Cold Blood* as a work of art and that treated the O. J. Simpson case as a soap opera to then turn on collectors of crime memorabilia as if they were, well, criminals."

What would Rick Staton say about this quote? He was at one time a leading collector of murderabilia in the nation and a foremost dealer in the trade. He once characterized himself as Gacy's "mule," so deeply was he involved in pushing Pogo's wares.

23.

Rick Staton warmly welcomed me into his Baton Rouge home. He looked much younger than his age, which I knew to be about fifty-five, give or take. He wore a bright yellow Hawaiian shirt, faded jeans, and white sneakers. His longish hair, dark brown tinged with gray, was slightly unkempt.

He gave me a brief tour of his home, a bungalow turned Gothic museum. In the foyer was a glass display case containing artifacts related to Ed Gein, including an antique jar that was buried on the killer's ghastly Wisconsin property, a letter he sent from the psychiatric prison where he did his time, and spooky photographs of the grave robber in his doddering old age. To the right were bookshelves crowded with true crime volumes, some of which were signed by their authors. Leaning amid the books were '80s Polaroid shots of Rick smiling beside a pale, bloated, and sullen John Wayne Gacy. The living room featured bins of old albums, mainly the surf music that Rick adored (think Dick Dale) and also some Zombies records with movieland monsters on the covers. Around the walls were vintage posters of monsters: Frankenstein's creature, the Wolf-man, Dracula. Also hanging was a painting by Joe Coleman, a friend of Rick's. It depicted Vietnamese prostitutes soliciting business in a squalid, sinister city. And then there were the relics and works of the killers—about fifteen hundred pieces scattered throughout the house, including a Miro-like paint-ing by Manson, a Gacy drawing of Rick's young son, a letter from Richard Speck (who murdered eight student nurses in one night), and a Christmas card signed by Bundy. Later I would see what Rick had hidden in his garage: nineteenth-century wooden coffins, small, designed for dead children, with glass windows to reveal their faces.

This was the sanctum of a true "gore-hound," as Rick later called himself. Clearly these morbid collectibles reflected a substantial part of Rick's being. He had been into horror movies from a young age and had even interrupted the honey-moon of his first marriage to watch the premiere of Hooper's *Texas Chain Saw Massacre*. He had written letters to some of the most heinous killers of our generation, regularly visited one of the most monstrous (Gacy) in prison, fielded many phone calls from psychopaths, and visited sites of terrible tragedy, including the Tate mansion. He had spent most of his adult life as a mortician, though he was now retired.

Rick's macabre compulsions did not make him dour. He was extremely friendly, high-energy, and funny as hell. Within minutes of our meeting, we were talking excitedly about hor-ror films (especially those of Bela Lugosi and Boris Karloff), old rock music, and the mortuary arts.

The conversation turned to murderabilia. Rick painted chilling portraits of the unrepentant Manson and Gacy; he gave a quietly respectful account of Elmer Wayne Henley, a deeply remorseful murderer who now creates somewhat accomplished landscape paintings; and he recounted tales of how people clamored for the wares he was selling—how thousands, some of them big-name celebrities, were willing to pay good money for the ridiculously bad art of hardened killers.

Schmid, it seemed, was right: though Americans on the whole vociferously condemn repetitive killers and the brokers who capitalize on their crimes, multitudes of these same moralizers—justified moralizers—are nonetheless fascinated by the monsters and their peddlers. As Rick said, many over the years have denounced his habits, but they're dying to see what he's got in his collection.

He knows why. Celebrity criminals like Manson and Gacy are, in spite of their atrocities, pop cultural icons, shapers of collective experience. They occupy places in our psyches next to JFK or Michael Jackson. To stand near a famous murderer, Rick confessed, was like touching history itself.

Celebrity can't erase the evil. Fame won't revive those murdered. Rick emphasized this. In spite of his desire to be close to the notorious, he recognized that the murderers with whom he had contact were the worst sorts of people: vile to the core, incapable of basic humanity. Rick loathed Gacy the most, finding the "Killer Clown" to be deceitful, selfish, childish, lewd, rude, trivial, petulant, cowardly, and dumb.

Over time, Rick's disgust with Gacy and those like him pushed him away from the murderabilia trade. He no longer wanted to associate with such malignant losers. But something else encouraged Rick to retire as well: the outrage of victims' families. Once Rick had a son of his own, he sympathized with the pain of those who had lost children to the killers profiting from his labors. He concluded that if he were the parent of a victim, he'd hate Rick Staton.

Rick now occasionally does freelance mortuary work, plays bass guitar for the choir in his church, and enjoys spending time with his son and his second wife. But he won't part with his collection. He still keeps coffins on the premises.

24

The day I returned from my visit with Rick, I received an e-mail from Joyce Carol Oates. I had written her earlier, asking for an interview, knowing that a response from this famous writer was not likely. However, Oates kindly replied. She said that she'd be glad to answer some questions via e-mail.

I'd contacted Oates because she's an expert on psychopathic criminals. One of her first important stories, the 1966 "Where Are You Going, Where Have You Been?" was inspired by Charles Schmid (no relation to the scholar David Schmid), a repetitive murderer known as the Pied Piper of Tucson. In the mid-'90s, Oates wrote a definitive essay on the psychology of serial killers that appeared in *The New York Review of Books*. And in 1996, Oates published a critically acclaimed novel called *Zombie*, told from the point of view of a man addicted to rape and murder. The story describes a person both morally reprehensible and worthy of sympathy.

I sent Oates five questions, imagining that she would agree with my basic assumption: that celebrity serial killers are psychologically rich revelations of our deepest fears and desires.

I was wrong. Oates ended her reply with this bracing corrective: "I am really not much of a 'romantic' when it comes to these subjects since I've written about them extensively; the more you know, the less enthralled you are likely to be."

Throughout her e-mail, her blunt realism countered my theoretical assumptions. When I asked her if serial killers occupied a place formerly held by saints—the trafficking of criminal "relics" suggested this—she had this to say: "No. This is just naive. Since I've researched & read about numerous 'serial killers' I know that these individuals are often brain-damaged, mentally unbalanced, not-very-bright, 'losers.' These are middle-school boys whom other students shunned or snubbed." Ironically, she added, if these socially challenged adolescents one day become celebrity criminals, "they will wind up being revered by some of the very people who'd avoided or laughed at them in school."

With a similar dismissiveness, she answered my Jungian question about the "shadow." I asked her if she believed that we should acknowledge the serial killer as a reflection of the dark side of our psyche. "One would probably say 'yes,'" she replied. "But this can be quite glib & superficial—the equivalent of people who claim, in quasi-intellectual fashion, that 'we are all Hitler'—some such shopworn cliché. It is much harder for people to acknowledge petty failings in themselves within their families, for instance, or within their professions; any grand gesture like recognizing 'evil' is likely to be just a gesture since it has no actual consequence."

For Oates, we in America are interested in these murderers not as disclosures of the shadow but out of a concern "with the detection, apprehension & punishment of criminals—there is a quite reasonable anxiety about any sort of criminal activity & especially the more heinous. Most of us imagine that we might be victims—not perpetrators. 'True crime' books or mystery/detective novels with satisfactory endings are what most people want to read." This idea recalled me to what I'll term the *Great Train Robbery* phenomenon: it's the excitement, the rush, that draws us to the morbid, the psychological and physical danger. (This was Pauline Kael's argument.) But there was something else in Oates's comment: a notion of justice; the satisfaction, often moral, of seeing rampant evil efficiently captured and punished.

Oates concluded, "You seem to be concentrating on superficial elements."

Was I obscuring petty human failings, the quotidian messiness of everyday life, with grandiose theories of evil? Was I unfairly downplaying the fact, rather uninteresting, that people like watching bad guys get caught and punished? After Oates's brusque responses, I feared I was. But I wasn't just afraid of that: for a few days I worried over whether this entire book was ill-advised, yet another expression of the academic tendency—relying too much on theory and not enough on experience—that I'd been trying to temper in my work. I felt embarrassed, too, over appearing naive, maybe just plain foolish, to one of the most celebrated novelists of our age.

I wish I could say that I overcame these anxieties by having a revelation that once more restored my confidence—an intuition disclosing the true nature of the morbid, say, or a discovery of ironclad evidence for Jung's theory of the shadow. Nothing of the kind came, though. The doubt, the insecurity, persisted (and persists).

What if I'm shallow? What if I'm missing the point? What if I'm dead wrong?

These are good questions for any writer—they check hubris and reveal blind spots. But a man, Hamlet-bound, can ask them too frequently; he can doubt himself into madness. How to counter exhausting skepticism with enabling faith?

Perhaps *that* is the question, more than whether to be or not. I can't answer it any more than the Dane could his, but I obviously muddled through my Oates-inspired nervousness to finish the book. One helper was Oates—I felt that her criticism saved me from dogmatism and opened me to complexities I had overlooked. Also, I kept reminding myself that a conclusive explanation of morbid curiosity—objective, substantiated with evidence, beyond question—was impossible for me to achieve. My book was not a treatise, after all, but an essay, an attempt, experimental in spirit, to account for my own experiences of morbid curiosity, with help from the ideas and research of others. How, then, could I be measured by standards of absolute right or absolute wrong? I was out for understanding more than truth: contemplation over "Q.E.D." If I were to wander into some wisdom, this would be welcome grace.

(I know: this is a very pretty justification for going forward in the face of doubt. It *is* partially true. But I also had a contract to fulfill. And I'm self-deluded enough to think that I'll be interesting even if I'm not quite right. In addition, my perverse imp sent me sick thrills, visions of actually being colossally wrong and publicly ostracized and going on a ferocious drinking binge and reveling in the decadent sweetness of just giving up—crash and burn, baby, all day long.)

So, for reasons good and bad, chastened yet resilient, and

hopefully with more sensitivity to nuance, I wrote, and here I return to Joyce Carol Oates, who, in addition to dashing me with cold water, does make a convincing point I'd like to consider further: We Americans are fascinated with serial killers because we thrill to their capture and punishment. Implicit in this idea is revenge—we want to make those suffer who made us hurt—but also the quest for justice, for morality. Perhaps we enjoy some morbid forms—television violence or horror films or celebrity downfalls—because on some level we are pleased that outright wrongdoers as well as annoying people get what they deserve.

25.

We take a moral pleasure in the criminal's just downfall. But we enjoy the falls of far less culpable figures as well. This is another form of morbid curiosity—our attraction to scandals, failures, descents from grace, and just the everyday clumsiness of the poor bloke who trips down the stairs.

I consider myself to be an educated man, but this doesn't stop me from reveling in stupid celebrity dish. I'm a little ashamed to say that I plunged into the muck of Internet gossip during the Tiger Woods sex scandal. Though I was disgusted by the remorseless rumormongering and flagrant mudslinging, I couldn't help myself. The cheaper the talk, the deeper I dove. My guilt only increased the glee. I wanted Tiger, an athlete I'd very much admired, to go down, weighted with ignominies from which he would never be free.

The feeling was similar as I dug into Mel Gibson's dirt—his drunken anti-Semitic rants and recent troubles with domestic violence. I also thrilled to the decline of Britney Spears, who rose to fame as a tantalizing blend of teen idol and sex icon, and plummeted with a highly publicized divorce, a shaved head and a shaved vagina, addiction problems, and an involuntary commitment to a psychiatric ward.

I go through long periods without following the scandals. A large majority of the population, it appears, does not. How else to explain the persistent media coverage of Paris Hilton, Kim Kardashian, Amy Fisher, Tonya Harding—women whose sole talent is flaunting decorum with forays into amateur porn? How else to account for the perpetual popularity of *Entertainment Tonight* and *Access Hollywood*? How else to make sense of the millions of readers of *Page Six*, *The Drudge Report*, *Gawker*, *TMZ*, and *The National Enquirer*?

Celebrities behaving badly, the Paris Hiltons of the world— these deserve mockery. But even as I join in the jeering, there's always in the back of my mind, as there was during my Tiger Woods voyeurism, a slight twinge of remorse: these people are human beings, just like the rest of us, and we should do unto them as we'd have them do unto us.

I've had this tension often. I don't want to run people through the mud; I love running people through the mud. Every New Year's Eve, I resolve to quit talking about people behind their backs, acquaintances, enemies, and friends alike. I stay true to the resolution for a week or two, but then I get with a buddy and we let loose: we make fun of almost everyone we know. There's nothing quite like unmitigated derision, becoming as nasty as possible, surreal and baroque with the insults, a geyser of spleen.

"It is not enough to succeed. Others must fail." Gore Vidal said that. The obverse, Vidal knows, is also true: whenever a friend succeeds, a little something in me dies.

26.

This is *Schadenfreude*. The term—German for "harm-joy"—signifies the pleasure we take in another's misfortune. Most would condemn this feeling, denouncing it as mercilessly morbid. But such contempt would miss nuances. That's what John Portmann would claim. In his book *When Bad Things Happen to Other People*, he explores Schadenfreude from an ethical angle.

According to Portmann, Schadenfreude is usually misunderstood as a vengeful mixture of envy and malice. You've got something I want, maybe fame or fortune, a skill or a higher rank, and so I envy you, and this envy produces a sinister yen to bring you down. I wish your failure. I'm certainly not going to cause it—I'm too moral for that—but I'll surely revel in it, should it come.

Such is the passive-aggressiveness generally associated with Schadenfreude: safe behind a façade of rectitude, we gloat over our friend's fall and might have actually spurred it on, albeit in subtle, unnoticeable ways.

Portmann saves the term from this negative interpretation. He uses it to describe the pleasure we feel when people get their honest comeuppance. We shouldn't feel guilty for this delight. As Portmann argues, sometimes our morose delectations are ethically appropriate.

Think here of Dante's notion of the *contrapasso*, the perfect punishment or reward for a crime or virtuous deed. As Dante's pilgrim makes his way through the *Inferno*, guided by the cool-headed Virgil, he initially pities the damned, especially Paolo and Francesca, buffeted about by filthy winds for all eternity merely for giving in once to their stormy erotic passions. In the theological scheme of the poem, the pilgrim's sorrow is not laudable; it shows a misunderstanding of a divine plan in which sin of all kinds should be loathed, not mourned. The pilgrim eventually leaves his pity behind. Descending deep into hell, he is disgusted by increasingly heinous sins and delights in justly applied punishments. His glee is a pious celebration of the moral structure of the universe.

A vision of the Christian afterlife is one thing, where all is perfect, pure, but this earthly realm is something else again—a muddled world in which justice is rarely separate from revenge, and the pleasures of justice are infrequently distinct from gloating. Still, isn't it fair to say that our pleasure in another's pain at least grows out of an impulse toward justice, even if this impulse is sometimes tainted by selfishness? Can we conclude that Schadenfreude is a healthy desire for fairness?

Maybe. But it seems to me that there's something much more "all too human" and much less perfectionist in Schadenfreude. I agree with Laura Kipnis; in *How to Become a Scandal*, she says that we like to "throw stones" at those scandalized because we enjoy "luxuriating in the warm glow of imaginary imperviousness that other people's life-destroying stupidities invariably provide." It's not that "Tiger deserves it"; it's "Thank God that'll never happen to me." The ecstasy of thorough self-deception.

What do we say, though, about the pleasure we take in watching someone whom we don't even know, probably more or less blameless, fall flat on his face? Do we fault a movie audience for laughing at slapstick—Keaton busting his ass, Moe poking Curly's eye? What to make of this malicious pleasure, which has nothing to do with public scandal and alleged justice?

27

In January 2002, the CCA Wattis Institute for the Contemporary Arts, in San Francisco, opened an exhibition called "Sudden Glory: Sight Gags and Slapstick in Contemporary Art." The works focused on falling—tumbling, spilling, slipping, and all the attendant embarrassments. In an interview, the curator, Ralph Rugoff, noted the archetypal descents—of Adam and Eve, of Icarus—but stated that his exhibition was attuned to the normal, everyday falling that "hints at our imperfect role in an imperfect world."

The show's title points to the merriment of watching another go down. It comes from the seventeenth-century British philosopher Thomas Hobbes (who sounds a bit like Kipnis): "Laughter is nothing else but sudden glory arising from some sudden conception of some eminency in ourselves, by comparison with the infirmity of others." Rugoff believes that this "sudden glory" is Hobbes's rendering of Schadenfreude, and that it highlights the "modest cruelty and sense of ridicule" that tinges our chuckles at the stumbles of our fellows.

Slapstick ruled Rugoff's exhibition, with Buster Keaton as

knockabout muse. Steve McQueen's video entry, *Deadpan*, showed the artist standing perfectly, insouciantly still as the wall of a barn fell down on him; luckily, as in the famous scene in Keaton's *Steamboat Bill*, an open window fit right over McQueen's body, and so he avoided being crushed. Helen Mirra likewise paid homage to Keaton; she taped all around one gallery's walls a strip on which was typed the script of the actor's masterpiece, *The Navigator.*

Other items in the exhibition included a series of photographs in which people throw themselves into the canals of Venice, and a film, *Mr. Pick-Up*, in which the artist John Pilson continually drops books, briefcases, and papers.

Why is all this funny?

In Woody Allen's *Crimes and Misdemeanors*, Lester, a pompous television producer, defines comedy. It is, he says, "tragedy plus time." He elaborates: "Oedipus, now, Oedipus, that's funny."

If you're watching Sophocles' *Oedipus Rex*, then you'll probably be moved by the gravity of the suffering and grieve for the fallen king. But if you're telling someone about the story long after the curtain has fallen, you might well find the narrative absurdly humorous. The tale contains wildly improbable mishaps (a man trying to avoid patricide and incest ends up, unbeknown to himself, doing exactly these deeds); jarring plot reversals (the king turns out to be a heinous criminal); irony (Oedipus bellows about how he'll punish the last king's murderer when he is in fact the murderer); and hyperbolic violence (Oedipus blinds himself with his mother's broach). All these could be elements of an especially black comedy, containing elements of farce.

The humor is dependent upon distance, and not just temporal. Certainly suffering can feel unreal because of its remote history. But the pain can also lack intensity for the reason that it's fictional, part of a drama—no one's really there to bleed.

Freedom from serious harm is essential to Schadenfreude unconcerned with justice. Keaton's character never gets permanently injured. Curly suffers no lasting effects. The same is true of all those unlucky folks on YouTube: "Funny Women Falling" (a personal favorite), "Funny People Falling," "100 Funny Falls," "Fat Guy Falls Off Bike," and "Fat Woman Falls Off Dirt Bike."

28.

Still, even though no one—at least to our knowledge—really gets hurt in these spills, can we justify our laughter, or do we conclude that it's just naughty and that's part of the pleasure?

We already know about the scapegoat theory: we take pleasure in violence perpetrated on another, because the victim allows us to purge destructive impulses. Though this theory seems most applicable to figures of serious violence, it helps to account for those more ordinary victims of slapstick, fictional or not. We laugh because we're glad to express the violence built up within us. It's the release of a pressure valve, a tiny effusion of aggression.

This idea is close to another, offered by Freud in *Jokes and Their Relation to the Unconscious*. Freud accounts for the maliciousness of many jokes by claiming that humor is a socially acceptable release of aggressive unconscious urges. For Freud, the unconscious is composed of aggressive and erotic urges; left unchecked, these would destroy civilization. But if these urges are repressed, they produce neurotic or psychotic behavior. Their most prominent release is sublimation, the transformation of negative into positive: a man's erotic instinct becomes a phallic skyscraper. Other, smaller leaks occur all the time, like jokes made at the expense of others. These allow us to enjoy, however superficially, taboo pleasures like sadism, and thus help us cope with obstacles to our unconscious urges.

Recent neuroscience supports Freud. A study published in 2004 showed that "altruistic punishment" of people who threaten a group fosters unity within that group. For one scientist, this finding reveals the "complex emotional dynamic of Schadenfreude"—we take pleasure in another's misfortune, even if it's not deserved, even if it's a mere accident, because the fall gives us a sense of community with others who are happy over the tumble. We know our friends by what they mock.

Schadenfreude will win you some buds—reason enough to enjoy, without guilt, the scandal. But guilt is more than half the fun. Have your guilt and expiate it, too. Now we're getting somewhere.

29

Sarcasm wears after a while. (Ask my friends.) Yes, there's a time to smirk sardonically at a celebrity's meltdown (Charlie Sheen's being the most recent) or a colleague's comeuppance. But what of someone who watches actual beheadings on the Internet? This is a different story. This is not aestheticized macabre, macabre at a distance, where no one really dies or even gets hurt too bad—not fictional or artistic or filtered through slicked-up media. This is a matter of real blood, real pain, real death.

After 9/11, beheadings of American citizens were made available to millions on the Internet. Take the case of Eugene Armstrong, known as Jack, a construction worker from Michigan who moved to Iraq because of the lucrative work opportunities there.

On September 16, 2004, only months into his stay in Iraq, Armstrong and two other GSCS employees were kidnapped by the Tawhid and Jihad terrorist groups, headed by Abu Musab al-Zarqawi. The terrorists claimed they would free the men if the United States would release the female prisoners from Abu Ghraib, an Iraqi prison being run by the American military. If the women were not freed, the terrorists went on to say, all three men would be killed. When the United States decided not to release the two Iraqi women incarcerated there—scientists allegedly involved in Saddam Hussein's weapons programs—the terrorists stayed true to their word. On September 20, they beheaded Armstrong. A video of the horrendous act was posted online. Over the next weeks, the two other hostages were decapitated, and videos were again uploaded.

The Armstrong video traumatized the world. Several masked terrorists stand behind him. He is kneeling. He wears a blindfold and an orange jumpsuit. One of the terrorists reads a statement demanding the release of the female prisoners. He finishes. The others hold Armstrong, and he slits the prisoner's throat with a knife. He then begins sawing Armstrong's bloody neck. The sound of squealing pigs in the background makes the scene more horrific.

Despite the appalling nature of this episode, millions watched the video only hours after it was streamed. Internet servers had trouble managing the traffic. More than half of these viewers lived in the United States, Armstrong's home country. Many millions more watched the beheadings of the other hostages. Seven years later, multitudes continue to view these and other beheadings on websites such as liveleak.com (formerly ogrish.com). These sites peddle a new genre of exploitation: war porn, video footage of actual beheadings and also of live combat, often supplied by the soldiers themselves.

One man, going by the pseudonym "John," tried to explain his obsession. "It's the thrill of quasi-participation, I suppose.

This is no horror movie. If it is titillation I feel, then it is because this is happening to a real person. The fear is real, the brutality is real, the blood is real, it is all real."

The viewing of grisly violence as an experience of bare reality—this is a prevalent assumption in the war-porn world. Ogrish.com once marketed itself with this blunt question: "Can you handle life?"

30.

At Christmastime, medieval Europeans staged beheadings, followed by miraculous revivals of those decapitated. This violent mimicry and subsequent resurrection, seemingly out of place with the Nativity, recalled bloody but holy episodes that had occurred close to Christmas: the stoning of St. Stephen (December 26), the massacre of the Holy Innocents (December 28), the martyrdom of St. Thomas Becket (December 29), and the circumcision of the baby Jesus (January 1).

But these beheading plays also echoed more primitive events, pre-Christian solstice rituals centered upon the sacrifice of a king. These rituals dramatized the murder of the old monarch (the waning year's symbol) and the installation of the new (the sign of the fresh cycle). Such practices were themselves vestiges of a much older ritual involving a real sacrificial killing of a king by his successor.

These sacrifices were related to world myths in which a murdered god brings life to the land. Think of the Egyptian deity Osiris. Through trickery, his jealous brother Set dismembers him. Isis, Osiris's sister and wife, puts him back together, but is unable to revive him—save for his phallus. She copulates with him, and the coupling produces Horus, the sun god who vitalizes the earth every spring. Dionysus's tale is similar. After the Titans tear him limb from limb, Zeus restores him and so ensures that the grapes will flourish. Jesus' death and rebirth also symbolize the seasonal cycle of decay and growth.

Are those millions now fascinated by war porn really, whether they know it or not, hoping to penetrate a deep mystery of existence, the merging of violence and creation?

31.

I've never watched the beheading videos. I'm too squeamish, afraid of a mental imprint that will disturb my waking and my dreams.

Jonathan Hayes wishes he had not seen a beheading. A forensic pathologist, he recorded his response to the video in which an American businessman, Nicholas Berg, is decapitated by the same group who killed Armstrong. Though Hayes had witnessed death many times, he regretted watching the Berg video. The violence, he said, "unearthed emotions I had no desire to feel: fury, despair, the desire for revenge. I no longer cared about the atrocities committed in Abu Ghraib, the images of which had outraged me the week before. I wanted every man in that little death club captured, torn from their families, and dragged into the darkest basement interrogation room."

Hayes admits that these feelings were inseparable from the post-traumatic stress disorder he was suffering from his work on Ground Zero in the immediate aftermath of the attacks. The video exacerbated his symptoms. It "crushed the necessary buffer between the abstract examination of a dead body and the pain and horror of that death" and so hollowed him with sorrow, causing him to break off a marriage engagement, retreat into isolation, and consider moving away from New York.

When does curiosity toward the morbid go too far and scar us for a long time? Hayes's article suggests that the lack of a "buffer" between a viewer and horrific images can damage equilibrium. Obviously, different viewers require different buffer zones. Some need large psychic areas between themselves and terrible sights; others, only a sliver. But without this buffer, we risk the transformation of morbid curiosity into trauma.

What is this buffer? The term implies a mental power that preserves the intensity of terror but keeps it from consuming us, that enables us to find meaning in the suffering, insight in the danger. For me, this faculty is the imagination. There are many ways to define the imagination, but one current that runs through the more intelligent definitions is this: Imagination is the ability to transform fact into symbol; that is, to turn raw existence into structures of significance.

The poet Samuel Taylor Coleridge explains. For him, the imagination relies on two processes, primary and secondary. The primary imagination is immediate perception of unadorned being; the secondary analyzes and synthesizes the unprocessed observation: "It dissolves, diffuses, dissipates, in order to re-create; or where this process is rendered impossible, yet still at all events it struggles to idealise and unify." This procedure requires self-awareness, that slight gap between what's going on and our thinking about what's going on. In that gap we can turn an unrepeatable, subjective encounter into an enduring representation that others can share. The ultimate result of this mental conversion: meaning. The singular becomes significant; the accidental, purposeful.

Coleridge offers an example of this process at work. He perceives a plant wavering in the breeze. He is moved by its greenish oscillations and imagines it breathing. He elevates this image to a meaningful concept: the plant is photosynthesizing, imbibing air and light, converting them into nourishment for itself and its environment. This physical concept he translates into a moral one: more than a respiring organ, this plant is a symbol for how we all should properly inhabit nature. We should be sensitive to its energies, take them in, transform them into nutriment, material or psychological, and in turn share our health with the world around us.

Not all events offer themselves as readily as breezy crocuses: some resist imagination. These are the moments that we can't comprehend, that we can't attach to systems of meaningful thought. These junctures can simply be weird, or they can be profoundly disturbing. Hayes found himself in the latter place. His viewing of the beheading overwhelmed his sense-making mechanisms.

Without imagination, morbid curiosity results in a shocking negation of meaning. But this same macabre inquisitiveness, bolstered by imagination, can generate knowledge. One can stand stunned and speechless before the horror; or one can imagine abomination as a significant, perhaps mythic pattern, burdened with tragedy but also illuminating the human condition.

The crime writer and scholar Harold Schechter believes that stories are essential for transforming macabre spectacles, otherwise shocking, into meaningful events. If I can assimilate a horrific eruption to a coherent narrative, then I can understand the terror as part of a larger and purposeful structure. Seemingly mindless violence becomes the predictable result of a story's beginnings and contributes significantly to the end.

This is the value of myth: it can convert the monstrous into the moral. Take the myth of Oedipus (not funny after all). A man accidentally kills his father and beds his mother and gouges out his eyes in remorse. The events aren't random, though; they are manifestations of divine destiny, revelations of cosmic order. Moreover, they send the message, Be humble before the gods. Or consider the story of Jesus. An alleged prophet is brutally and unjustly crucified, but the atrocity is an integral part of God's plan and an admonishment to believers: You, too, must be willing to sacrifice yourself when the deity calls.

There are less grandiose examples, of course, of how we imagine narratives to console our sufferings. We understand a serial killer's ostensibly random brutalities when we connect them to tales from his troubled childhood. We come to terms with nature's deadly disasters by saying that the human suffering, appalling, teaches us how fragile life is and that we should take nothing for granted and try as best we can to help and love one another.

32.

He saw it all. If he'd stayed on the muddy ground—it'd been raining all morning—he would have been lucky to get even a glimpse. He was only sixteen and so had not reached his full height, and in any case it was chaos down there—thousands, all straining, pressing, to get close to the scaffold. But perched on the tree limb, he had a clear view: eye level with the victim, though she couldn't see him through the white hood.

The instant he heard the executioner pull the bolts—the sound of a hammer striking wood—he knew that he would remember this until he died.

She was middle-aged but, as everyone had remarked, remained youthfully beautiful, with full, lustrous hair, and a graceful bearing. She had an excellent figure, too. He could see that through her dress—black silk, thin, tight, clinging, because wet, to her skin.

She started her ascent to the scaffold. He felt ashamed of his attention to her body, and tried to think of something else. Why had she walked from the prison to her place of execution?

Why refuse the courtesy of the carriage? Why trudge through rain and mud?

A sign of bravery, aloofness even—to expose herself to the gawking of this throng. She reached the platform. She stared straight at the rope, walked directly to it, and faced the crowd. She never closed her stoic eyes or looked down while the executioner bound her hands and then her feet. He pulled the cloth down over her face and placed the noose around her neck.

The rumor was that she would get a reprieve. The day it had happened—three weeks earlier—she found her husband, John, in bed with another woman. Rage erupted, then violence: at first only in words, a vicious quarrel between a husband and wife, but then in action. She took a swing at him, missed. He retaliated by striking her with his riding whip. Fleeing the next blow, she saw the axe near the hearth. She grabbed it, wheeled around, and swung as hard as she could. She heard the skull crack and knew he was dead before he hit the floor.

Maybe if she hadn't lied to the police, telling them that he'd been kicked by a horse . . . She stuck to this fabrication almost until the end, even though the evidence said otherwise, and this unwillingness to confess probably turned the home secretary against her.

The charge was murder. She was convicted. The punishment: the accused, Martha Elizabeth Brown, was to be executed by hanging, on August 9, 1856, in the county of Dorset.

The bolts slammed, the door opened, she fell. There was no cracking of bones: just a thud. She didn't die at once, but writhed, like a fish on a hook, for at least a minute. Then she went limp, and slowly swayed, a grim pendulum, and eventually became still, and forever fixed in the mind of the sixteen-year-old, an architect's apprentice named Thomas Hardy.

When he was eighty, and internationally famous for his esteemed novels, Hardy could still vividly conjure the image, with a mixture, disturbing to some, of the morbid and the erotic. In response to a letter from a woman living near Brown's village, he admitted that he was "ashamed" to say that he witnessed the hanging, his only excuse being that he was but a youth. What he remembered most, he continued, was "what a fine figure [Brown] showed against the sky as she hung in the misty rain, and how the tight black silk gown set off her shape as she wheeled half round and back." He emphasized his fascination with the dead woman's comely appearance in another late reminiscence, this time told to a young interviewer. What he recollected most clearly, Hardy confessed, was the "rustle of the thin black gown the woman was wearing."

We probably don't find it strange that a curious teenage boy would be attracted to a public hanging. What likely does give us pause, though, is Hardy's lust toward Brown's suspended corpse. Sure, love and death have perennially been intertwined, in hyperromantic contexts—I want to die with you so that our love will live forever—as well as more orgasmic ones (think of the French "petite mort"). But Hardy here seems to go beyond these typical confluences, and even beyond the more Gothic sensibility of Poe, who said that the most "poetical topic" in the world is "the death of a beautiful woman." Hardy goes necrophiliac: this dead woman was hot.

33.

Hardy's morbid eroticism might well be just as normal as anything else: the intense attraction any of us might feel toward
violence sometimes resembles the carnal urge. Still, normalcy
doesn't make it right. It's exploitative to reduce suffering to sex.
There was a real woman up there on that scaffold, with a
unique history that included family, love, joy, pain, insight, er-
ror, stupidity, unfairness, anger. To flatten her to an object of
sensual pleasure is inhuman, torment reduced to porn.

This is J. G. Ballard's theme in his novels *Crash*, from 1973,
and *The Atrocity Exhibition*, first published in 1970 and reprinted
in an expanded version in 1990: how the failure of feeling causes
macabre eroticism. Bored with traditional sexual pleasures—
the thrill of a beloved's touch—we require shock to get off: a
limb-mangling car crash turns us on, or the gruesome assassination of a president. Most of us are rightly ashamed when we
harbor such monstrously insensitive lusts, but that doesn't stop
us from looking, especially under the protection of righteous
outrage. We vociferously condemn photographs in which Amer-

ican soldiers force Iraqi prisoners into sicko porn poses; at the same time, we're dying to ogle the images.

This mingling of Eros and Thanatos, sex and death, as creepy as it appears on first glance, is perhaps inevitable. Sexual arousal and fascination with death have much in common: both are extremely stimulating, often uncontrollable; primitive, taboo, irrational, and ecstatic, pushing us outside our habits into the intractable mysteries of creation and destruction, and their inextricable connection. On the other hand, though, death is death—putrid, gross, stagnant—and life is life—green and fresh and lithe—and never the twain shall meet, and it's perverse to try to blend them. Moreover, it's also dangerous, this confluence between lust and destruction, since it can reduce those who suffer—the sick and the dying—into commodities and can thus result in "non-caring which will have negative survival value for our species," to quote, again, Professor Jack B. Haskins, who condemns all macabre curiosity.

It's surely significant that I waited until now, halfway through the book, to mention the lascivious side of morbid curiosity. I've had such troubling erotic desires, and I'm embarrassed by them, and would rather not bring the matter up at all. (A Southern Baptist upbringing dies hard.) The sex is out in the open now, though, and it was a Victorian, of all people, who flipped on the light. Let's face it: one source of macabre fascination is carnal. I'll admit the objects of my prurience if you will.

As a boy, I had a thing for Carolyn Jones's Morticia, the Gothic matriarch in the 1960s sitcom *The Addams Family*, based on Charles Addams's *New Yorker* cartoons. She had a pale complexion; long black hair; a shapely figure revealed by her form-fitting gown, also black; a dark sense of humor; a fixation on dead things; and a robust horniness, barely disguised by network mores, for her husband, Gomez. (John Astin, the lucky actor playing the spouse, later claimed that "Gomez and Morticia were the first married couple on television who seemed actually to have a sex life.")

Jones's Morticia is only one of many sexy Mistresses of the Night, ranging from Maila Nurmi's Vampira, ghoulish babe turned horror show host, to Dita von Teese's more recent Glam Goth persona, blending bondage fetish, old-style burlesque, and haute couture. In between, pop culture has been haunted by many such macabre seductresses, most of whom don't really do it for me (Cassandra Peterson's Elvira, for instance, or Anjelica Huston's big-screen Morticia) but some who emphatically do (such as Carrie-Anne Moss's *Matrix* character, Trinity, dressed in black leather, shiny and skin-tight, and Christina Ricci's spookily captivating Katrina in Tim Burton's *Sleepy Hollow*).

Nothing wrong with a middle-aged man finding the playful eroticism of these eerie seductresses attractive. But there is something rather unseemly, most would agree, in getting aroused, as Hardy did, over a dead woman's body. Nonetheless, I remember experiencing a sexual charge when I first saw the bluishly luminous, spectrally angelic, exquisitely Poe-esque corpse of Laura Palmer in David Lynch's *Twin Peaks*. Who killed her wasn't really as important as seeing her dead.

So I'm perverse. I'll bet you are, too. The world's gone

necrophiliac, especially when it comes to vampires. *True Blood*, *Twilight*, *Underworld*, *Blade*, *Buffy*, *Interview with a Vampire*—wildly popular, sexed up all to hell, teeming with pallid, scantily clad hard bodies sure to turn you on regardless of your gender or sexual persuasion.

Is there a way to transform pornographic morbidity—carnality toward the macabre gone selfish, insensitive—into a sentiment more noble? The story of Thomas Hardy answers yes. Hardy was honest enough to admit his lasciviousness, his lust toward another's hurting, and in this confession was the beginning of a great transformation: of sick thrill into subtle art—nuanced, empathetic, and charitable. Scholars agree: Hardy's experience of Brown's execution was the inspiration for *Tess of the d'Urbervilles*, maybe his most powerful novel. Tess kills a man who once raped her and has hounded her for the rest of her life. Though her deed is understandable and possibly justifiable, Tess is convicted of murder and hanged.

Through Tess's story, Hardy explores the relationships between fate and freedom, justice and injustice, action and irony. Did a cruel or indifferent universe determine Tess's sad tale, or is she responsible for her tragic end? Is justice served in Tess's execution, or is it unfair for an innocent to die just for looking out for herself? Are there any deeds in this world that aren't ironic—intentions that aspire to one result but in fact produce the opposite?

Hardy's imagination empowered him to transcend his immediate response to the macabre, callously erotic, and discover deep significance in the morbid occurrence. He elevated eros into ethics, fact into symbol, catastrophe into rich and enriching narrative. In doing so, he revealed another origin of macabre fascination, one that adds to the erotic and transcends it, to a region more generous: attraction to the morbid event can spring from an admirable desire to contemplate life's most meaningful mysteries—love and death, and their vexed connection.

34.

When I teach nature poetry, like that of William Wordsworth (in whose former house, in Racedown, an elderly Hardy once recalled Brown's hanging), I emphasize distance. If a poet is too close to the scene he's describing, then obviously he won't be able to see clearly the textures, contours, color. All he'll perceive is a blur—just as you will, right now, if you press this page right up against your nose. Likewise, when a poet is too far from his landscape, he'll lack clarity of vision as well—such as you will, if you walk several feet from this page. You won't be able to read a word.

Lucid perception, as any nature poet or landscape painter knows, requires the middle distance, a perspective that can attend to the parts—a whorl in bark, the leaf's serrations—without losing a sense of the whole, and can conceive of the whole—the oak's trunk and the cirrus clouds—without being ignorant of parts. In this perceptual median, understanding thrives: the disparate portions make sense as integral units of a harmonious ensemble, and this ensemble's complexity comes to light in the portions.

You know all this right now, as you (hopefully) move back and forth smoothly—almost imperceptibly—between the marks on the page and the meanings they compose. This effortless vacillation is successful reading. Perusal fails when one side or the other overwhelms: when you struggle simply to grasp definitions or syntactical relationships, or when you are so consumed by one idea that you skim the pages that don't address it.

Witnessing Nicholas Berg's beheading, Jonathan Hayes found himself, conceptually speaking, too close to the macabre—the gruesome event was too particular, confusing, indecipherable—and the proximity traumatized him. He lacked a sufficient buffer, the imaginative distance that would have enabled him to connect the raw fact to larger meanings.

This is the result when imagination, as the ability to create significant mental structures, falters: all is a bewildering blur. But what about imagination becoming too robust, excessive, imperious? Then one swings to a position opposite to that of Hayes. The witness becomes overly confident of his ability to understand an event, morbid or otherwise. He brings a prefabricated idea to a disturbing experience, with the smug confidence that this notion will allow him to comprehend the event, sort it out once and for all, connect it to this meaning and this only. But he's deluded, insensitive; his conceptual arrogance actually alienates him from the episode, puts him at too great a distance. He can't see the trees because he's too engrossed in the forest.

To focus on forest and trees equally, comprehension and complexity, idea and individual: this is the golden mean of successful imagination. Hardy achieved this median when he elevated his vexed experience of a hanging into a powerful, capacious meditation on suffering. Someone beholding the sublime—maybe Burke or Kant—reaches this middle ground as well, getting close enough to a catastrophe to sense its potency but staying far enough away to be free of harm and able to glean meaning.

But to confront the morbid without imagination or with too much, too close or too far: blankness results. We forgive the former situation—who hasn't had his mind shut down in the face of a beheading or a hurricane? We usually condemn the latter, however, because it is often the product of prejudice. We find this reductive thinking (obviously) in the egotist, the racist, the fundamentalist, but also in the hard-core Marxist, or feminist, or capitalist—in anyone who flattens phenomena to a preconceived idea and thus turns individuals into ciphers of a system: allegorical figures that point to an abstraction. (In Joyce Carol Oates's mind, I was oversimplifying in just this way in my thinking about serial killers and society, and I hope her criticism has saved me from being too blindly rigid.)

Morbid eruptions invite this sort of dehumanizing. Exposed to terror—the hurricane or the decapitation—we often rush to a well-worn, uncomplicated worldview that makes the situation seem familiar, and so assuages our fears. But this defense mechanism, even if its presence is quite understandable, divorces us from reality. It encloses us in the shell of our idea. Wherever we look, we see ourselves only.

This cognitive narcissism, often unwitting, is at work

whenever we exploit the suffering of another for our own pleasure, turn a person's hurting into a commodity we consume for our pleasure. This dehumanization, unredeemed by proper imagination, has been vividly on display in a recent cultural development: the rise of the fight club.

35.

In a twilight schoolyard, a shrill throng surrounds two shirt-less boys. They look to be sixteen. Awkwardly, they swing at each other, rarely landing a blow, until they lean together, exhausted. As if suddenly horrified by this closeness, one roughly pushes the other away. The boys now stand three feet apart, facing, breathing hard. The crowd calms.

The quiet quickly ends, though. The horde screams: *Kick his ass!* But the two don't move. They glance guardedly from side to side. Then they fix on each other, almost sweetly. The boy on the right remembers why he's there. He resigns himself, puts up his fists, shuffles toward the other, who hesitantly puts up his guard.

Before the one on the left can get ready, his attacker strikes him with a right hook. The boy staggers; the aggressor tackles him, straddles his chest, hammers fists into his face. Within seconds, eyelids flutter: a knockout.

The winner springs up, raises his arms. He looks around. It's now dark. He stares into the mob. Somewhere in there is a girl he knows, his age. There are older people, adults, men and women (one holds a toddler). There are children, too, junior high age or younger, flushed with joy and terror.

This brawl wasn't a spontaneous, ephemeral scuffle between two classmates. It was deliberately planned, and the opponents were strangers. And it was far from transient. It was filmed so that it could become part of an underground video called *Agg Townz Fights 2*. The boys fought their hearts out to participate in a growing phenomenon around America's suburbs: teen fight clubs recording their bouts for profit. The clubs' organizers sell the homemade DVDs on the Internet or in back alleyways. Videos that don't make it to market are often posted on YouTube.

The legal authorities in Arlington, the city where the 2006 film was shot, were understandably troubled by these deliberate acts of assault and the illegal trafficking of the videos. The law acted, and those who profited from the DVDs are now in jail.

While this fight club ring was broken up, similar operations exist today, in 2011, in New York, New Jersey, California, Washington State, and Alaska. No doubt other states have the problem as well, even if the authorities have yet to address it. What puzzles many is that these instances of teen savagery generally don't take place in America's poorer neighborhoods, which historically have higher rates of violent crime. Fight clubs are mainly on the rise in middle-class and upper-middle-class environments.

Cultural critics have complained. Orin Starn, an anthropology professor at Duke, claimed that these clubs manifest a grimly nihilistic "part of the American psyche fascinated by the spectacle of blood and violence." For Starn, the staged battles are products of "the *Mortal Kombat*, violent video game generation," offering youths "the chance to bring those fantasies of violence and danger to life—and maybe have your 15 minutes of fame in an underground video."

But the man whom some see as the dark source of these clubs offers another perspective. Chuck Palahniuk, author of the 1996 novel *Fight Club*, which served as the basis for the popular 1999 film, had this to say about the violent teens: "God bless these kids. I hope they're having a great time. I don't think they'd be doing it if they weren't having a great time."

Is a boy attacked and beaten down by a total stranger having a good time? Should we bless a young man eagerly watching the beating and doing nothing to help? Don't we want to condemn those who witness the pain of others for their own pleasure? I imagine, though of course I can't know this for sure, that most gawking at these staged fights—like most watching war porn—are probably just out for a quick distraction, anything to keep boredom away. For fans of fight club videos—as I'm envisioning them—the battling boys aren't intricate humans, hopeful and vulnerable and desperate and lonely and a little brave; they are especially interesting machines, programmed to entertain.

I view the audiences of these videos negatively because I believe that the fights actually encourage exploitation. The fighters present themselves as commodities and those watching play the consumer. Human beings disappear: all that's left is quantity, a price tag. Numbers blot out bruises and cuts.

(I sound self-righteous—as though I'm above getting a

cheap thrill from watching a filmed fight. I'm not. When doing research for this book, I wasted more than one afternoon guiltily gaping at street fights on YouTube.

I'd like here to differentiate between morose voyeurism (my occasional vice) and morbid curiosity. Morose voyeurism is the reduction I've been exploring: of individual to idea; pain to price. Morbid curiosity, as I'd now like to define it, is the opposite: it's an eager, open-minded interest in the macabre—disease or destruction or death—as a special invitation to think about life's meanings. For this kind of curiosity to yield meditative fruit, the imagination must be active: imagination as Hardy embodied it—as the median between voyeurism, on the one hand, and confusion, on the other, between too far and too close, whole and part.

36.

A girl no more than eleven stares at you. Her blue eyes are wide, curious, inviting. There is an impish quality to them. She might relish mischief—that harmless sort small children enjoy, tying a gaudy ribbon around a cat's neck or good-naturedly taunting a friend when he trips.

This little one is the picture of innocence, not that sentimental kind that views children as angels but that more Wordsworthian type: the child as premoral, neither good nor evil but ignorant of both, not yet thwarted by self-consciousness, still spontaneous in affection and anger, simply existing as she exists, in the moment, like a mockingbird or a wave.

The girl's overall appearance is charmingly careless. The bangs of her black hair—cut just above her shoulders—are parted slightly in the middle. She is enigmatically grinning, Mona Lisa–style. She wears a pink blouse buttoned up to her neck, with a wide collar flaring over a soft, unbuttoned black sweater. Her green plaid skirt, knee-length and pleated, suggests the starched propriety of a school uniform; but this decorum is offset by her red socks, bunched up over her Mary Janes. The bare knees tell the story. They are bruised a little, scabbed, and a Band-Aid covers a small wound on the right leg. This is a girl who likes to play outdoors, forgetful of her body, keen on fun.

On a second look, though, we see that the knees are genuinely battered. Maybe there was a serious accident. And her white skin is a bit too pale; she looks sick.

She exists in a painting twenty-two by twenty-eight inches. She stands tall in the middle, the focal point, with her eyes first striking the attention. Surrounding her in the rectangular frame are pictures hinting not at innocence but horror. To the left of her head is a small scene of her strangling another girl. Below this image and a little to the left is a mother lying on a hospital bed, recoiling from a baby the nurse holds above her. To the left of this, a skeletal creature bears in its arms an infant of its own. The baby reaches desperately toward the sky while the grotesque parent gnaws one of the baby's hands. Above this nightmare, in the upper left-hand corner, is a boy's face, underneath which is a caption: "Kip Kinkel."

Other scary images crowd the portrait, closing in on all sides of the girl, with written passages crammed among them. The overall effect is repulsive but also beautiful—a compelling blend of sweetness and monstrosity.

The painting is by Joe Coleman, a Brooklyn artist. It's called *And a Child Shall Lead Them*, and it depicts, in image and word, the story of Mary Bell. She was born to a prostitute named Betty in 1957, in the British town of Newcastle-upon-Tyne. The father was unknown. Betty, whose specialty was sadomasochism, tried to kill her unwanted daughter on several occasions. She used strategies that would make the death look like an accident.

Her primary scheme was to leave strong pills where her toddler could easily access them. One time, Mary ate so many iron tablets that she lost consciousness and had to have her stomach pumped. Eventually Betty put her child to use, forcing her, as early as the age of four, to perform sex acts with her johns, especially fellatio. The mother would push her daughter to her knees—this is why they are bloodied—and hold her head back. Grown men would force their penises into her mouth. She would gag on the semen and vomit. There were other terrors. Betty would punish Mary for wetting her bed by rubbing her daughter's face in the urine. She would then hang the wet sheets out the window, adding public embarrassment to the physical mistreatment.

These forms of abuse contributed to what happened on May 25, 1968, the day before Mary's eleventh birthday. Two weeks earlier, a three-year-old cousin of Mary's, Martin Brown, had been discovered near some abandoned sheds, his head bleeding. Later Mary admitted she'd pushed the boy off a ledge. On her birthday, Mary took this violence further. She strangled Martin to death and left his corpse in an empty house.

A short time after, Mary brought a friend, Norma, to see what she had done. The girls then found Martin's aunt (not, as far as I can tell, Betty's sister, but a more distant relative to Mary) and told her that her nephew was lying dead. After the funeral, Mary and Norma continued to visit the aunt, repeatedly asking her how much she missed Martin. The girls also called on Martin's mother, June. Mary asked if she could see Martin. When the grieving mother protested that her boy was dead, Mary said she wanted to see inside the coffin.

Mary engaged in yet other incriminating behaviors—it

seems as though she wanted to be caught. One night, she broke into a nursery near her home. She trashed it, and left behind a note: "I murder so that I may come back." Mary also sketched a picture of a boy lying in the same posture as the dead Martin.

These details came out to the police much later, in August, after Mary, never apprehended for Martin's murder, killed again. This time, with Norma as an accomplice, Mary strangled Brian Howe, another three-year-old. The crime took place on July 31. When police found the corpse, they were shocked. Here was a dead toddler, partially covered with weeds. Beside him lay a pair of broken scissors. His genitals had been skinned, and his thighs were pocked with puncture wounds. Some of the hair on his head had been chopped off. His belly had also been lacerated, probably with a razor. The wound was shaped like an M.

Once more, Mary behaved as if she wanted to be apprehended. She and Norma suggested to Brian's sister, Pat, that they knew where her missing brother was. Pat never found the body, but the police did, and they quickly gathered evidence pointing to Mary and Norma. When they questioned Mary, she didn't admit to the killing but, while trying to attribute the crime to an eight-year-old, described the scissors perfectly. Since this part of the crime scene was then known only to authorities, Mary betrayed her connection to the killing. She gave herself fully away on the day of Brian's funeral, August 7. As the coffin was being carried from the boy's house, Mary was watching. She broke into laughter and rubbed her hands together in a sinister fashion.

The police arrested her and Norma, charging each with two counts of manslaughter. Norma was acquitted, but on

December 17, 1968, Mary was convicted. She avoided the murder charge "due to diminished responsibility." The jury agreed with the court psychiatrists—Mary had exhibited classically psychopathic behavior and thus should not be deemed fully accountable for her acts. During her imprisonment leading up to the trial, she had spoken as if she didn't understand remorse. At one point, she said, "Brian Howe had no mother, so he won't be missed." Another time, she claimed, "Murder isn't that bad, we all die sometime anyway." She also stated, "If you're dead, you're dead, it doesn't matter then."

37

I knocked, the door to the Odditorium opened, and there he was: Joe Coleman. He wore a black vest across which dipped, just above his waist, a watch chain bearing a silver cross; a black coat hanging down almost to the knees; a black necktie; a white-collared shirt; black pants; and black boots. His dark hair was slicked back. He had a long, bushy goatee and a thick mustache waxed upward at each side. This was a man from another century, the nineteenth, and he had seen strange things.

We shook hands and he asked me in. Would I like some wine? Yes, I said, and he disappeared into an adjoining room. I was alone in the dimness—there were no windows, and somber crimsons absorbed the low light. And in this gloom were creatures, covering almost every inch of wall and floor: life-sized wax people, and severed heads and hands, also of wax. There were jars containing deformed fetuses; bones; death masks; coffins; gadgets I couldn't recognize; urns.

I'd read about Joe's Odditorium and so expected an on-slaught of freakishness—Ripley's Believe It or Not on acid, a circus sideshow worthy of Roderick Usher. But I wasn't ready for this melancholy weirdness. For an instant I felt that I was trapped inside a sick man's head, among others who had ventured into this skull and transmogrified into tormented objects. I got a little panicky.

Joe returned with coffee mugs full of red wine. He handed me one, walked over to a large canapé made of bizarrely carved and painted wood, and, before sitting down himself, offered me a small folding chair. I took it and forced myself to focus on the interview, to avoid gawking at the baroque freakishness crowding the room.

Over our four-hour conversation, fueled by cup after cup of wine, Joe held nothing back. He answered my questions—I had pages of them—with energy and clarity, patiently unfolding his ideas, often pausing for long periods to consider the next word. His deliberate clearness, his obvious comfort with his own being, stood in stark contrast to my own nervousness and tendency toward pedantry. (I found myself constantly quoting other writers and invoking arcane academic theories. For some reason, in order to emphasize the conceptual heft of some of my terms, I kept saying things like: "She's innocent with a big *I*," or "That's life with a big *L*." What I should have said is that I'm a phony with a big *P*.)

We ranged over a wide variety of topics, beginning with David Lynch and film noir, progressing to Ed Wood, diverting to Jim Thompson, slowing to consider America's crisis in faith, moving to the nature of television, speeding up through a litany of outsider artists, such as Henry Darger, and registering Joe's discomfort with being labeled in this way. And these are only a few of the issues that we discussed. Still, one idea unified our heterogeneous talk: to attune oneself to the power of darkness is, as Joe put it, to clear the static from your soul and open a "dark channel" that can carry you close to God. "You get more connected to God when you go to the darkest place."

We turned to Joe's painting of Mary Bell. One purpose of the work, Joe said, was to convey the fact that "innocence and evil can occupy the same little child—every human child, not just Mary Bell." All children feel victimized by the world, and possess enough anger to take revenge against the very fact that they exist.

This is what it means to be a child, but also an adult. "All of us are Mary Bell," Joe asserted. "Inside [of us] is a little kid . . . all of humanity are children. In God's eyes, we're all children." And we all are born "with tragic flaws, sometimes physical, sometimes deeper." There's no such thing as a normal body, a perfect body, except in an anatomy chart. Humans are imperfect, broken, weary, alienated, and it is the artist's calling to find beauty in the pain. "Painting," Joe said, "is pain."

Anguish awakened Joe to his art. Abused by an alcoholic father, bullied by other children, inaccurately diagnosed as retarded, Coleman grew up consumed with rage, and could easily have turned into a Mary Bell himself. But instead of directing his violence toward others, he expressed it in his art. (Although he did once try to set his elementary school's playing field on fire, and he developed, at fifteen, a habit of barging into the houses of strangers and exploding himself with fireworks taped to his chest, an act he would repeat as an adult performance artist named Professor Momboozo.) Mostly the young Coleman transformed his anger into drawings of the ghastly final hours of Jesus' life. As he matured as an artist, he developed more sophisticated ways of venting his brutal impulses, either through his shocking one-man performances, which often featured, in addition to explosions, his biting the heads off rats, or through his paintings, bluntly honest explorations of his destructive energies.

Joe calls his violent performance art the way of the shaman, an embodiment of "internal chaos no words [can] describe." His painting he terms alchemy: he delves into his inner agonies as a magus would descend into dark earth, and he finds gold in the gloom. Joe calls his painting style "internal digging." He wears jeweler's glasses, the better to detect the subterranean networks.

Joe's art is indeed a mirror of his deepest being. Obsessed with doubling—he was born on 11/22/55 on 99 Ward Street in Norwalk, Connecticut—Joe uses his painting, regardless of subject, to reflect his own demons and angels. Take his picture of Mary. Completed soon after Joe married Whitney Ward (a name suggestive of doubling) on November 11, 2000 (or 11/11/00, another repetitive figure), the work was probably inspired, as the writer Katharine Gates suggests, by his "darkest fears that love can conjure up, feelings of anxiety about reproduction, as well as the horrors of potentially reenacting one's own childhood trauma through the relationship." Notably, Joe and Whitney have decided not to sell the painting. They keep it in their home as their "symbolic offspring."

Joe expresses his paternal care by painting the child in his characteristic way: by placing her at the center of an expanding series of contexts, growing from the most particular to the most general, each shedding fresh light on her complex life. His method is "circumferential," to draw from Emily Dickinson's description of her way of apprehending the world: a concentric sort of perception where the object rests at the center of increasingly capacious circles of comprehension.

This perspective exemplifies proper imagination. Imagining Mary thus—as a site of intricate significance—Joe goes much deeper than Hardy in showing how morbid experience can provide enlivening insight. Where Hardy turns one macabre occasion into an indirect inspiration for a scene in one novel, Coleman makes the morbid the central theme of his art. With rigor and passion, he deliberately translates life's terrors into both his mentor and muse.

One way Joe illuminates Mary is to feature in his painting bits of text from James Hillman's psychological study *The Soul's Code*. Hillman claims that some people are born to crime, regardless of environment, and argues that these "bad seeds" should not be stifled but challenged to express their dark energy in healthy rituals, such as the creation of art. Joe's painting also includes a poem written by the young Mary, intimating that this morbid little girl, with proper guidance, might have turned into an Anne Sexton or a Sylvia Plath. There are also in the work passages from the Gospels, in which Jesus asserts that the child is most likely to enter the kingdom of God; behind the obvious irony of these citations is the idea that Mary's story, viewed as a revelation of the mysteries of darkness, might well be redemptive.

Other images offer additional circles of understanding. At Mary's feet are a bloodstained Harlequin, whose costume blends black and white, and a soiled white teddy bear, with a clock in its belly and an artificial candle hoisted by its right hand. The Harlequin encourages us to think about relationships between good and evil, innocence and experience, while the bear encourages thoughts of time and eternity as well as of darkness and light. Yet another circle of vision is Joe's border that really isn't a border. Although certainly the rectangular frame encloses the teeming portrait, it also gestures toward other incidents and ideas. At the bottom of the frame, for example, are images of an erotically charged Mary in prison and of JonBenét Ramsey, another innocent subjected to adult lust and violence. Together, these pictures force us to consider the Freudian conjunction of Eros and Thanatos, love and death.

As Joe and I came to the end of our interview, I felt that we were at the core of a growing Gothic universe. The Odditorium forms that earlier hid in crepuscular obscurity became clear. Strewn seemingly pell-mell throughout the wine-dark sanctum were a life-sized figure of Fidel Castro, made of wax; a document signed by Ted Bundy; a large likeness of Charles Manson, with a bloody knife in his hand; the skeleton of a baby; a Tibetan monk's skull; a reliquary containing the remains of Christian saints; a two-headed pig floating in formaldehyde; an actual mummy, in full, from the pre-Columbian age; a misshapen baby named "Junior," also in formaldehyde; a wax figure of a Chinese man being eaten by rats; the death mask of John Dillinger; a life mask of Charles Laughton; a taxidermist's rendering of a two-headed prairie dog; two miniature mermaidlike figures from Fiji, named Gretta and Eddna and made of monkey skulls, antlers, and human hair; a lamp whose shade is an armadillo's shell; a jar containing removed tumors; and leg braces constructed for polio victims. The tenebrous energy of these specimens flowed through the partitions dividing Joe's museum from the other apartments, and spilled out into the city night.

38.

In one of his lectures, "From Darkness to Light: The Mystery Religions of Ancient Greece," Joseph Campbell says: "I'm reminded of a picture showing the figure of Death playing the violin to the artist. Let Death talk to you and you break out of your ego pride. That means you've got to put your head in the mouth of the lion." A poet with his head thrust far beyond the fangs was John Keats, who in his "Ode on Melancholy" asserted that death and beauty are one: we can experience the comeliness of a creature only when we realize its mortality. A beautiful mistress—with a "peerless eye"—or a rainbow of the "salt sand wave" or the "wealth of globed peonies" or the "morning rose" dwell "with Beauty—Beauty that must die; / And Joy, whose hand is ever at his lips / Bidding adieu; and aching Pleasure nigh, / Turning to poison while the bee-mouth sips."

Horror and unwholesomeness and dying call us near the world's wonders. The fever kills but makes the countenance glow. This is the meaning of Wallace Stevens's line "Death is the mother of beauty." This is Dickinson's "ecstasy of death."

William James explores this macabre vigor in *Varieties of Religious Experience.* In this psychological study of the sacred, he distinguishes between the religion of healthy-mindedness and the meditations of the sick soul. Those who hold to the religion of wholesomeness believe that God has created a world that "is absolutely good," and so faith equals positive attitude. In contrast, the sick soul believes that the cosmos is as evil as it is good, a place of suffering as much as joy; he thus often falls into pessimism and melancholia, moods he finds more authentic than lighter ones. To this ailing soul, "there is no doubt that healthy-mindedness is inadequate as a philosophical doctrine, because the evil facts which it refuses positively to account for are a genuine portion of reality; and they may after all be the best key to life's significance, and possibly the only openers of our eyes to the deepest levels of truth." Morbid contemplation is an article of faith.

During the European Renaissance, scholars kept skulls on their desks. Clocks from long ago and even today bear the motto *Tempus fugit*—time flies. Soon after the advent of the daguerreotype, late-nineteenth-century Americans and Europeans commissioned images of their recently deceased loved ones; these postmortem pictures might be miniatures to be cherished while abroad, or they could be bigger, designed to rest on a nightstand or shelf.

These practices exemplify a perennial motif: *memento mori*—literally "remember death," often translated as "remember you must die." The message is double: Don't take the things of this world too seriously—your riches or your success—because all will soon rot; care passionately for each instant, for your duration on earth is short and you need to make the most of what time you have. What to ignore and what to value, which experiences are vital and which are not: death can teach us this rare wisdom.

A famous scene in Shakespeare's *Hamlet*—the prince holding Yorick's skull—illustrates this idea. (I know it's almost a cliché to invoke this example here, but I can't help myself, so perfect is the image. I'm also obsessed with the play—a cliché as well, I'm afraid, for someone who would write a book like this.) Staring at his jester's skull, Hamlet broods over how all earthly success—even that of Caesar—crumbles to dust. At the same time, he implies what he will later claim: to experience most fully an irreducibly evanescent world, one shouldn't rest in static conclusions but remain flexible, dynamic, sensitive to the scope of each moment. "The readiness is all." In the next century, Thomas Gray in his "Elegy Written in a Country Churchyard" observes that "the paths of glory lead but to the grave," a statement that mocks the vanity of worldly endeavor while urging readers—as Robert Herrick earlier encouraged virgins—to "make much of time."

On an earth ineluctably ambiguous, fraught with doubt and complexity, death is the one sure thing. Most of us live in denial of demise, and virtually assume immortality. I know I do. I waste thousands of hours surfing the Internet for stupid information or updating my Facebook friends (rather narcissistically) on my latest bike ride. I ignore my parents, my spouse, my friends, my child, imagining that I'll express my true affection for them tomorrow, that I'll spend time with them tomorrow, that tomorrow I'll slow down and stop taking them for granted. I neglect myself. Instead of delving into my uniqueness, I lazily become an echo chamber for cultural commonplaces, an exponent of the mass. I increasingly use clichés. I rot my brain watching too much TV.

A world catastrophe, or a stranger's passing away, or the violent death of a young friend, or a child's horrific end—these can shock me out of complacency. This is what the philosopher Martin Heidegger would conclude. Shivered by the deaths of others, we are forced, he argues, to stare at our own mortality: If it happened to them, it can happen to me. In this moment, I might become authentic, realizing that no one can die my death for me; in my dying, I am an unrepeatable entity, different from everyone else, a period to an existence that I alone carried out.

Death's perpetual certitude inspires us to imagine more truthful lives. But death, by thwarting narcissism, also elevates our ethical imaginations. What does the egotist believe but that his existence is more important than those of others, that his self is of immense value and preeminently worthy of being nourished and perpetuated? Death deflates this puffery, positing that all attempts to boost the "I" are ultimately vain. Though you are unique on one level, on another you are the same as everyone else: you will suffer and die and return to the dirt.

Shaking us out of narcissism, death calls us to merge with our fellows, to enter into a global community bound by hurt. It says: You are dying, and this is pain, and you would like to alleviate it in any way possible, and so now you apprehend the plight of all others, also moribund and agonized and in need of succor. Obviously, when we experience this distress, we don't by necessity become aware of the miseries of others. We can hurt selfishly, convincing ourselves that our discomfort is worse than anyone else's and thus deserving of the most care. But hopefully we will, when we realize that our lot is common, suffer charitably, and so translate our own groaning into empathy with another's torment.

One gains this close knowledge only through the imagination's capacity to go outside one's skin. In his "Defence of Poetry," Percy Bysshe Shelley elaborates: A "man, to be greatly good, must imagine intensely and comprehensively; he must put himself in the place of another and of many others; the pains and pleasure of his species must become his own. The great instrument of moral good is the imagination."

Minding the macabre, we imagine truth, we imagine the good. We also imagine, as we know from Keats, the beautiful. Why is the real rose more handsome than the porcelain? The living one is finite, decaying, bound to die, and the mortality produces the luminousness.

The reddish bloom bursts from a tangle of greenery. You are arrested by the lusty crimson. You can't stop looking. You recall your dead mother's flower garden and nostalgia wells up. This strangely pleasant yearning intensifies when you notice a black spot on one of the petals wavering before you. The rose is disappearing, and you desire to hold to this moment, to make it stay, appreciate it as deeply and for as long as you can.

What if I told you that you had one year to live? You would be riven to the core, undone by thoughts of all that you'll miss. But you would become desperate for life, seeing every second as painfully precious. The world would become more vivid than ever before, more beautiful.

These broodings on death are a bit sentimental, and rather commonplace. But sometimes clichés crudely express collective longings and powerful truths.

39.

I know a man named Nowell Briscoe. He lives in Atlanta. He is an elegant old-style Southerner, well-mannered and evocative of sonorous August longings and Harper Lee. He's also a total hoot, ritualistically sipping mint-tinctured gin-and-tonics (G and T's, as he calls them) while waxing lyrically over the sublimities of vampire movies and *Hush . . . Hush, Sweet Charlotte.* For the past fifty years he's been collecting obituaries.

Nowell's archive, contained in more than thirty thick plastic binders, includes national newspaper eulogies of celebrities he admires, major Hollywood stars like Bette Davis, for instance, but also such lesser lights as Richard Todd, who played the preacher in *A Man Called Peter.* He also preserves death notices of interesting strangers he has come across—a beloved teacher who reminds him of his own high school history instructor, or a man so eccentric that he sported a walrus mustache and pince-nez glasses in 2009. He also has in his files obituaries of people from his hometown, Monroe, just outside Atlanta. Most important, the collection holds the three obits most precious to Nowell, the first three he cut from a newspaper and pasted into a book: those of his grandfather, grandmother, and aunt Ruby.

When Nowell was seven, his grandfather died. This was the boy's first encounter with death, and he was confused and sad. His dad called him up to the big leather easy chair in the den and read to him the obituary, which focused on his grandfather's benevolent influence on friends and acquaintances. The young Nowell immediately felt better. The ugliness of dying and death's finality, terrible as they were, had produced a gentle tribute to his family's beloved relative, a description of what was best in his life. In the words, his grandfather came richly alive: cogent, glistening, eternal. The boy had never loved the man more.

Nowell had a similar experience when his grandmother died soon after, and then, three years later, at the passing of his aunt Ruby, a town librarian who had introduced him to the lovely world of books.

Ruby—generous and smart, gifted in wit, with movie-star good looks in the black-and-white photographs that grace Nowell's walls—saved the boy from a lonely childhood. Too tall for his age, physically awkward, the young Nowell didn't fit in well with his classmates. Ruby noticed this, and invited him, when he was ten, into her realm: volume after colorful volume, all containing universes in which a sorrowful and solitary youth could find lovely domains. As Nowell told me, Ruby was his true mentor and muse, and so her death, from a heart attack brought on by diabetes and kidney disease, almost destroyed him. Her obituary, which he pasted in an elegant green leather scrapbook she had given him, is a thing of beauty, a memorial in which his aunt still breathes, cracks wise, and guides.

Especially sensitive to grief, to its pains but also its affectionate disclosures and comforting memories, Nowell grew up to become a mortician. He chose this vocation, he confessed, because he wanted to help people when they were most in need. He also cherished the power of mortuary art, able, like an obituary, to transform a corpse, often disfigured, into a form comely and unforgettable.

He's retired now from this work, and calls himself the archivist of death. But he is full of life, galvanized by reminiscing and keen on what has not yet passed—*True Blood* and brisk cocktails and good conversation and also good books, lots of them, such as Allan Garganus's *Oldest Living Confederate Widow Tells All*, one of his favorites. He has turned the underworld into his paradise: rot into rose.

40

I once got lost on the battlefield of Gettysburg. The historic site, now contained within the Gettysburg National Military Park (which covers some eight hundred acres), was within walking distance of my hotel room. The first morning of my visit, right about dawn, I made my way there. I had never been much of a student of the Civil War, but I had recently read Joshua Wolf Shenk's *Lincoln's Melancholy*, and had been eyeing, high on the shelf in my office, Shelby Foote's multivolume history of the conflict. And so I was curious about the place so important to the war's outcome, possibly more for the soaring Lincoln rhetoric it inspired than for its military history.

By the time I left the ground, a massive cemetery, with more than a thousand monuments to the dead, ornate language was not on my mind.

I was alone on the narrow roads connecting the rolling hills, whose late-April dew shined in the day's first light. In the sun, I read the epitaphs on the stone memorials scattered throughout the fields. This Confederate regiment fought here, this Union one skirmished there, a general fell under this tree, a brave lieutenant got wounded near this rock. Death was every-where.

I got that uncomfortable feeling: I'm on the verge of falling into a History Channel kind of reverie, a mental reenactment, filled with hackneyed heroism and suffering, reminiscent of the very bad art on a set of commemorative Civil War plates. And I got embarrassed, wondering if I'd ever get rid of my maudlin tendencies, born of reading too much lachrymose poetry and Hamlet worship. Then I felt another urge, a cool steel counter to all the weepy sepia: to mock both myself and all the pomp of war memorials.

Before I could get started, a scene flashed in my mind. Sandi and I had given our daughter, Una, a new scooter for her seventh birthday. Within a week, the scooter had disappeared. Appar-ently she had left it outside overnight and someone had taken it. This was only the latest instance of what I saw as my daugh-ter's inability to take responsibility for her things, and so, instead of comforting her—she loved that scooter—I berated her, tell-ing her how disappointed I was that she was so immature, that she wouldn't take proper care of her stuff. She began to cry, and she said, "I'm the worst girl ever." I held her and reassured her. It was too late. She was inconsolable, and remained so for much of the day. I could have been charitable but had not, ne-glecting, even with a small gesture, to ease my girl's suffering. I had missed an opportunity for affection that I would never have back. Here was time's excruciating, chronic "too-lateness." Only death is prompt.

The graveyard had turned uncanny, as Freud meant the term: a site where sensations long repressed in the unconscious return as both strange risings (they'd been forgotten) and familiar feelings (they've been integral to the self). This tension was uncomfortable, tinged with anxiety over my emotions' powers and fraught with guilt over my inadequacies, but also a prod to understand pain and how to alleviate it.

41

Not interested in Disney World or Paris, lush mountains or pristine beaches, millions of people each year plan their vacations around places like Gettysburg, desolate areas where tragedies occurred. Those spending their vacation dollars on visits to Auschwitz or the New Orleans neighborhoods ruined by Katrina or the rubble of Ground Zero are known as "dark tourists."

In his introduction to a collection of scholarly essays on the subject, Richard Sharpley admits that people have always been attracted to places of death; however, this sort of journeying has notably increased in the last fifty years, probably because the tourism industry as a whole has grown. The opportunities for this kind of vacation are many and diverse, and not just guided tours of the Katrina damage. You can visit the site of the Chernobyl nuclear reactor disaster, or the London Dungeon, replete with medieval torture exhibits. Or you might consider a trip to Cambodia's Tuol Sleng Genocide Museum, located in the infamous Security Prison 21, where the Khmer Rouge regime committed some of its worst atrocities. Another popular destination is Mumbai's Dharavi slum, the largest in Asia and the focus of *Slumdog Millionaire*, the Oscar-winning film. And then there's the Pennsylvania farmer who charges sixty-five bucks to see the cornfield where Flight 93 went down on 9/11. If you're not sure where to go, you can check out www.thecabi net.com, which maintains a regularly updated list of dark tourism opportunities.

How to feel about dark tourism? Is it a crass commodification of another's suffering, a sort of tourist porn? Or is this kind of travel an effort to understand another's torment—to empathize—and thus to gain a fuller knowledge of the human condition and a stronger desire to behave generously?

During a visit to Louisiana in the summer of 2010, my wife, Sandi, was kind enough to help me with the research for this book. While I was interviewing Rick Staton, she took a post-Katrina tour, one of many such opportunities in New Orleans, including not only posthurricane excursions but also cemetery tours, voodoo tours, and ghost tours. A knowledgeable guide drove Sandi and six others to the Ninth Ward and its environs, telling detailed stories about the disaster and the city's slow recovery.

The guide, a New Orleans native, was living in the city when Katrina hit. Like so many, he evacuated, leaving his home to watery destruction. When he returned to his neighborhood after several weeks in Texas, it was devastated. Formerly flooded houses still stood empty, their furniture and carpets ruined, mold corroding their walls, and food rotting in refrigerators long unpowered. The stench was overwhelming. Soggy photographs and other beloved keepsakes littered the floors. The streets were strewn with lonely objects: a tricycle or a cracked terra-cotta pot or a baby doll. The atmosphere was ominous, the guide said. There was an abiding fear that unclaimed corpses, putrescent after days of exposure, were lying in alleyways not yet explored. As the guide drove the group around the areas most damaged by Katrina, now and then he pulled to the side of the road to cry.

The tour awakened Sandi to the crushing grief of Katrina and its aftermath. Near the end of the day, exhausted and raw and tender, she found herself tearing up when the guide wept. The tragedy of New Orleans had come to harrowing life for her, and she was transformed, a melancholy witness to suffering that earlier, when depicted on TV, had seemed so far away, almost unreal.

Once the five-hour tour ended, Sandi lingered for a while, talking to the guide. She felt a connection with him, wanted to know more about him. He freely told her more about his experience of Katrina. She confessed how much his tour had affected her, how her heart was brimming and her eyes opened. She then confessed her reason for taking the tour, and told him about this book.

He understood the positives and negatives of dark tourism immediately, and had a story. The only unfavorable evaluation he had ever received from a client, he said, resulted from unmet expectations for gore. A man on the post-Katrina tour had complained that he hadn't seen enough devastation, destroyed buildings and abandoned cars and the like. This person, the guide said, embodied the worst in tourists: indifferent to misery, out for petty thrills.

According to the guide, since Katrina, dark tourist opportunities in New Orleans have been on the rise, and visitors increasingly grumble about the lack of real disaster. They treat tragedy like an amusement park ride.

Sandi's experience and that of the unsatisfied tourist mark two extremes. Facing a city apocalyptically wrecked, Sandi had her imagination expanded and her emotions stretched, while the malcontented tourist had felt little and thought less.

I'm not saying that my wife is a better person than the disgruntled traveler. I'm pointing to the distinction to highlight the value of dark tourism—it can stimulate the imagination toward exceptionally dynamic empathy—as well as the problem with it, which is that it encourages the reduction of suffering to a commodity.

Which factors lead to the former and which to the latter? Certainly the presentation of the tragic events has something to do with the experience—is the "packaging" respectful or exploitative? A person's disposition is decisive, too; some people are just more emotionally sensitive than others.

But ultimately, I can't figure out why one person's transformation is another's disappointment. What I can say is this: the fact that multitudes are now touring morbid New Orleans and other grim destinations suggests that humans are drawn to witness the worst, and that one powerful source of this attraction, hidden in some people and overt in others, is the hunger for truth (we all die), beauty (we had better appreciate living things while they last), and goodness (we all suffer, so let's comfort one another).

42.

What, Susan Sontag wonders, is a proper reaction to another's suffering? In *Regarding the Pain of Others*, she asks whether photographic representations of another's agony, no matter how well-intentioned, can ever transcend exploitation and produce authentic, ameliorative empathy. She acknowledges that certain images—such as the "snapshot of the little boy in the Warsaw Ghetto in 1943, his hands raised, being herded to the transport to a death camp"—can function as "objects of contemplation to deepen one's sense of reality; as secular icons, if you will." But this kind of encounter is unlikely, if not impossible, in our contemporary culture, which in general lacks the "sacred or meditative" spaces conducive to genuine thinking and feeling. Most of our public spaces are megastores or airports or museums—places not meant for seriousness.

Sontag believes that depictions of suffering even in the most reverential museums are cheapened by babbling tourists, busy educational programs, and crowded walls. She wonders if pictures in a book might represent the pain of others more effectively. At least one usually looks at a book in private, and so is more likely to apprehend the hurting. But the time with the book will end, and the intensity of the emotion, regardless of its initial force, will fade.

The problem isn't only exploitation. It's also our emotional response. Most of us try to whip up sympathy in the face of harrowing pictures. But as Sontag argues, "the imaginary proximity to the suffering inflicted on others that is granted by images suggests a link between faraway sufferers . . . and the privileged viewer that is simply untrue, that is yet one more mystification of our real relations to power." Sympathy in fact removes us from the agony, because it is based on the idea that we "are not accomplices to what caused the suffering."

For Sontag, only when we set aside sympathy—assuming we've already rejected sentimentality, the romanticization of suffering—can we potentially reflect on how "our privileges are located on the same map as suffering and may—in ways we might prefer not to imagine—be linked to suffering, as the wealth of some may imply the destitution of others." It is possible, though unlikely, that the images of the pain of others might supply an "initial spark" to this shouldering of responsibility.

How does this sharing of responsibility occur? I've said that morbid curiosity—as opposed to traumatic shock before the horrific and to reduction of the gruesome to commodity—can be a muse to empathetic imagination, which isn't the ability to feel *for* someone in pain (this is sympathy) but the capacity to feel *with* the tormented person, to achieve emotional unity and like intensity. Practicing empathy, one elevates to what the theologian Martin Buber called an "I-Thou" connection, in which the beholder, by way of charitable imagination, opens to the complex, unique fullness of the beheld, and grasps, if only for a second, what it's like to exist as *this* being and no other and thus what this person (or creature) requires for its thriving and how, with labor, to grant it.

Moments of such imaginative intimacy, I'm sure Sontag would have agreed, are extremely rare, maybe even nonexistent. But does it matter if this transcendence lacks palpable reality? Can't it stand as an ideal toward which we generously aspire, an inaccessible goal that nonetheless calls forth actual deeds that make us and our world more alive?

In *A Portrait of the Artist as a Young Man,* James Joyce, through his protagonist Stephen Dedalus, suggests that this kind of empathetic transcendence, infrequent though it might be, is possible. It occurs when we become unselfishly attuned to permanent sorrow. Stephen focuses on tragedy, the aesthetic devoted to suffering. He agrees with Aristotle: the tragic inspires fear and pity. However, Stephen thinks that Aristotle neglected to define these emotions sufficiently. He proposes to do so.

He draws a distinction between aesthetic and nonaesthetic fear and pity. For Stephen, these emotions lack aesthetic power—they are not beautiful—when they are kinetic. Pity can decline into a desire for the shallow pleasure of self-satisfaction. "Look at those poor African children; I'm glad I'm not in their place, and it sure makes me feel good to send them money." This fall into egocentrism is pornographic, a reduction of the suffering into an object to be consumed. This inclination is kinetic because it is a movement *toward* something. Fear can likewise become degraded; it can turn into mere loathing, an impulse to move *from* a phenomenon. "The images of African hunger show the world's terrible injustice; I blame capitalistic greed for this, and denounce this economic system as evil." When this revulsion occurs, fear is didactic, a self-righteous disgust toward what offends. The kinetic—the nonaesthetic—comforts the ego, reassuring it with conventional sentimentality or prudery, and alienates it from actual pain.

In contrast, a proper aesthetic encounter, though static in nature, throws us into the suffering: it disarms the narcissist's pornography and didacticism and frees pity and fear to be what they should be. Correct pity, or tragic pity, doesn't evoke sentimental yearning for a pained object but "arrests the mind in the presence of whatsoever is grave and constant in human sufferings and unites it with the human sufferer." The legitimate fear inspired by tragedy is also connective. It doesn't induce aversion from the fearsome event. Instead, it "arrests the mind in the presence of whatsoever is grave and constant in human sufferings and unites it with the secret cause." In both cases, the beholder of the event elevates from particular to general—from the unique torment of this unprecedented moment to the enduring gravity of the human condition. The viewer realizes that he is fundamentally linked to this episode. Through pity, he suffers with the person in torment; through fear, he understands the terrorizing powers. He comprehends victim and victimizer both, the agony and his implication in it.

When the witness achieves empathy with the object—which can be verbal or visual or aural—he recognizes it as an "esthetic image." Such an image possesses three qualities. First, it strikes the beholder as a cogent, discrete event, "selfbounded and selfcontained," unique in its emergence from "the immeasurable background of space and time." It shines as just *this* image, and nothing else. It has integrity, *integritas*. With this awareness comes another: the unity is not simple but a gathering of disparate parts into a dynamic harmony. The image, though one, is also many, a coalescence of complexity. It has consonance, *consonantia*. Together, unity and diversity generate radiance, *claritas*: revelation of the object's inmost essence, the fullness and force of its identity. Encountering this threefold brilliance, one undergoes "the luminous silent stasis of esthetic pleasure, a spiritual state . . . [an] enchantment of the heart."

43.

Tragedy and darkness create tranquil light. Sontag's cautions still resonate, though. I wonder if I'm overly sentimental (a recurring fear, as should be clear by now), dangerously romanticizing suffering to satisfy my ego. I've been imagining pain as a phenomenon that is not meaningless but a path to wisdom and goodness and beauty. Am I trading harrowing fact for poetic fantasy? Am I trying to assuage guilt over my own ethical shortcomings by convincing myself that my writing about the hurting of others—absent my deeds to assuage it—exonerates me?

In spite of my doubts, however, I persist in my belief: the morbid offers illuminations brighter than the sun. Great souls have preceded me in this conviction. They are negative theologians, and their basic principle is this: Darker emotional states—doubt, confusion, alienation, despair—inspire a deeper and more durable experience of the sacred than contentment does. When we are bereft of secure beliefs or psychological clarity, tormented by guilt or nostalgia, we often give up hope. But in relinquishing this hope, and in teetering near nihilism, we also give up our expectations, those frequently egocentric desires that we project upon the world in our attempt to control it, to make it familiar and safe. With these coordinates gone, we find ourselves floating in emptiness, unmoored. We open ourselves to a power strange to that realm. When this force seizes us, we feel—we do not think—that it is what we need to salve our agony.

The Cloud of Unknowing, whose author we do not know; St. John of the Cross's *Dark Night of the Soul*; T. S. Eliot's *Four Quartets*; the letters of Mother Teresa, in which the revered woman once wrote, "If I ever become a saint I will surely be one of 'darkness'": these are only a few of the more notable instances in which a spiritual seeker has drawn on negative theology in describing his or her quest for divine union.

No knowledge, no joy, no solace, no love, no life. To this devastating realm of the "not" you must go for salvation, a tearing asunder of all that you value, where your being is almost totally erased. Only then—nothing but a paltry vapor—can you be brought back to vigor and know, in your nerves, the spirit of life, as Lazarus understood blood only after having his capillaries freeze.

44

When I was thirty-five, only weeks after Una's birth, I closed myself in my study and imagined blowing my head off with my father's old shotgun. It was April. The sun had just gone down but the blinds were still closed. I didn't want light. It was utter darkness I desired, complete negation. I knew the gun was in the basement, tucked behind the furnace. All I had to do was go below, and that would be it. But I couldn't get up. I heard my baby crying in another room. She was hungry, and I knew I should go help my wife feed her, but I didn't care. I lacked the volition to cause my own death, and the love required to give life. This was worse than hell. It was limbo's listlessness. I was apathetic, and apathetic about being apathetic.

There was more than one night like this around the time Una was born. Instead of being anxiously hopeful, I was neither dead nor alive. I had fallen into a depression so deep that I could scarcely move, much less take care of my little daughter.

My form of depression was (and is) bipolar disorder. It has pulled me apart, between gloomy indifference and a manic struggle to *make* my life meaningful. The one side, the despairing one, says: Why bother with anything, with writing or taking a walk? Nothing matters. The other side howls: Wrench every second into some purposeful endeavor.

This condition flared violently when the responsibilities of fatherhood threatened the coping habit I had developed over the years: distracting myself by holding to an obsessive, exhausting work schedule.

I woke every morning at four, wrote for three hours, took a one-hour run, and then rushed to my office, where I wrote, conducted research, or taught until six in the evening. When I returned home, I slammed the booze, five drinks a night, or more. I needed the anesthesia of alcohol to tranquilize my perturbed nerves and ease my guilt over being such a poor husband.

By the time I reached my mid-thirties, I had published three books and had two more under contract. I had also published numerous articles in scholarly journals, well into the twenties. I had given around thirty talks at conferences. I had been invited to lecture at good universities. I had received awards— from my own university and the National Humanities Center. I was granted early tenure, then promoted early to full professor, and given an endowed chair.

I was addicted to success. It suggested to the world that I was mentally healthy and thus gave me an excuse not to do anything about the dark moods that alienated me from those who might love me and whom I might love. What I didn't realize was that this hunger for accolades was a symptom of my disorder, the mania manifesting itself, usually as a counter to the depression always threatening to suck all volition.

Una screamed into my life. She disrupted my work habits, and I was forced to realize that I was an extremely sad, troubled

man, pitifully trying to convince himself that he was perfectly
fine and certainly not in need of help or affection.

Exposed, I felt worthless. I seriously considered suicide. I
told myself that my daughter would be better off without me,
that my sickness would pollute her.

Sandi was painfully attuned to my deadness. She was married to a zombie, and knew it, and had endured this numbness
for years. She loved me, she said, and it would break her heart,
but she was determined to leave me, for her sake and our daughter's, if I didn't seek help.

Life without Sandi and Una, alone and alcoholic and a
stranger: this blunt reality stirred me, just slightly, from my
stupor. I reluctantly agreed to counseling.

I forwent one-on-one therapy—which I'd tried before with
little success—and entered a group. This form of therapy
requires stark honesty that often foments heated exchanges.
Wishing to avoid conflict—and not really wanting to face my
own problems—I remained mostly silent during the first few
weeks. When anyone criticized my reticence, I said something
blandly agreeable.

Then I was exposed and broken.

On this night, I was catatonically depressed. I said nothing
and stared at the floor. With about ten minutes to go, one of the
female members, during an awkward silence, blurted: "It's Eric
I worry about the most. I wouldn't be a bit surprised to read
about him in the papers one morning. He's the kind who stays
quiet, puts on the fake grin, does his work, but then one night
blows his head off."

No one is ready for it. An outburst from a woman I barely
knew did what my wife's beseeching and my baby's crying could

not. It penetrated to the very root of my darkness—my hopelessness and failure to love and my loneliness and my slow cruelties.

I sobbed. Tears burned my cheeks. Snot oozed into my mouth. I might've wept for ten seconds or an hour; I might have been in the room or Jerusalem.

When I returned to an awareness of my surroundings, I considered bolting for the door. But the woman who had expressed her concern gently handed me a nearby box of Kleenex. I cleaned my face. I looked around. Everyone was waiting.

I confessed, desperate to be absolved. I said I was selfish and arrogant, a terrible father and husband, and, worst of all, suicidal.

I expected the group's support and affirmation. What I got was a look of restrained rage from one of the younger women in the group. She told how her father had neglected her. He was an alcoholic and always either too drunk to give a damn about anything other than his own pleasure or too hungover to care about anything but the next drink to ease his pain. He never told her he loved her. He sometimes forgot her name. He died of liver failure and left the family destitute.

Her father's neglect had deeply damaged her. She had been in therapy for years but remained depressed. She had nothing good in her life.

She continued to glower. She leaned forward. She spoke directly to me: "Do you want your daughter to turn out like me? She will, I promise you that, if you don't change your ways right now. Every second you're not showing her all the love you have, you're not doing right by her. Every second is precious but you're living like you've got twenty lives and a million chances. You get one chance, and it's now, and you're fucking it up."

The therapist said time was up. The woman rushed out. I followed, but she was gone before I could catch her.

I stood alone on the dim sidewalk, afraid to take one wrong step. Everything counted, every single instant. And I had been living as though there were numberless opportunities for sharing affection and I would live forever and have infinity to get it right.

That disturbing night was a rarity: a true turning point. As I walked home alone after the session, I realized that I had granted my illness lordship over me. In viewing my depression as a despot subjecting me to its savage fancies, I was able to escape responsibility, to indulge fully my selfish desire to let my ego flourish unfettered, not obliged to anyone. But this wasn't freedom. It was a prison—a cell separating me from those who cared for me and for whom I should have cared.

The scales fell from my eyes. I pledged to myself, with an urgency I'd never known before, to cherish my daughter and to recover, somehow, adoration for my wife.

I'd made such vows before, but I'd failed to keep them. This time, however, I found a good psychiatrist who gave me my current diagnosis (bipolar II, mixed) and prescribed appropriate medications. He recommended a skilled psychotherapist who convinced me of the importance of taking responsibility for my mental illness.

As I adapted to the medications and struggled with the lessons of my therapist, I rather fortuitously, one winter morning, came across a passage from William Blake. This was in 2006, when my daughter was three. The lines were as follows: "Mutual Forgiveness of Each vice, / Such are the Gates of Paradise."

I understood that forgiveness need not be simply the letting go of anger; it can also be a way of seeing that opens us to bliss, that cleanses the "doors of perception," as Blake puts it elsewhere, and perceives the world as it is: infinite, exquisite. Forgiving requires that we put aside our egocentric concerns and attempt to witness and embrace the real.

From that day onward—buoyed by effective drugs, supported by excellent psychotherapy, and catalyzed by fatherhood—I have labored to *forgive* my manic depression, to relinquish my negative judgments toward it, to cease viewing it as a tyrannical taskmaster ruining my life. This effort has liberated my bipolar disorder to be what it is: not a curse but a part of me, no different from my hands or auricles or larynx, an element of my constitution, no more and no less.

Stripped of its dark powers, the disorder has emerged as more than an affliction. I can see it now as an indispensable energy in the shaping of my identity, of my flaws, yes (such as an obstinate narcissism), but also of my productive sensibilities: my love of contemplation, my honesty about life's troubles, my willingness to endure confusion and discover solutions.

And my manic depression has also revealed to me what I most need to be alive: the vulnerability that inspires the giving and receiving of affection. Doing so, my condition has shown me the requirements of fatherhood and beauties of my daughter.

Una is now nine years old. She has become a good singer. When the year turns to fall, she plays soccer. She loves the exuberantly morbid stories of Roald Dahl. When she calls me from my study, I answer and walk through the door.

45.

This was my dark night of the soul. I had fallen to that depth that Melissa Febos reached: blackness so destructive that I knew, if I were going to live, that I had to draw strength from "a God of some kind." This is how Febos described her descent and the first sparks of her rising in *Whip Smart*, her memoir about her addiction to drugs and S and M that almost killed her.

The morbid nadir carries traces of the apex. Kay Redfield Jamison, in her memoir *An Unquiet Mind*, claims that *because* of her bipolar disorder, not in spite of it, she has "felt more things, more deeply; had more experiences, more intensely; loved more, and been more loved; laughed more often for having cried more often; appreciated more the springs, for all the winters; worn death 'as close as dungarees,' appreciated it—and life—more; seen the finest and the most terrible in people; and slowly learned the values of caring, loyalty, and seeing things through."

Loren Rhoads, editor of *Morbid Curiosity*, a magazine devoted to "true stories of the unsavory, unwise, unorthodox, and un-usual," expresses a similar idea. For her, fascination with the unwholesome is "ultimately life-affirming." We are more alive when we face what we can't quite understand—on edge and required to think beyond our habits. This is the value, she says, of traveling in the dark: there is always risk, but it provokes unprecedented acuteness.

This is the abiding value of melancholy, and, sometimes, of depression, if the depression isn't too debilitating or suicidal. Some will of course call melancholy and depression harmfully morbid, emotions that sever us from health and love and life. But the morbidity of sorrow—not cultivated sorrow, but that which comes inevitably—is often a productive sluggishness, a time when the soul slows down, too weary to go on, and takes stock of where it's been and where it's going. During these gloomy pauses, we often discover parts of ourselves we never knew we possessed, talents that, properly activated, enrich our lives.

Don't stay in the sun too long. Keep a skull on your desk. Or, just when the winter slush dissolves and there is one daffodil, look around for a rugged cross.

46.

There is much to mock in modern Christianity: sweaty televangelists arguing the infallibility of a book written thousands of years ago by disparate, biased authors; self-righteous school boards attacking modern science; crazed fundamentalists calling for public burnings of the Koran; unwittingly campy producers creating annual passion plays that blur Christian rock, cinematic violence, and blissed-out New Age hokum.

Then there's the weirdness of the religion. It asks its believers to eat, during communion, its God. It expects young adults, in spite of natural cravings, to abstain from premarital sex. It encourages its faithful to worship a freak of nature, a zombie.

But brilliant thinkers and artists have embraced this religion. Even if we put aside the great negative theologians and other past sages—including Augustine, Aquinas, Pascal, Anne Bradstreet, Blake, Kierkegaard, and Gerard Manley Hopkins—we are left with an august list of recent Christians: T. S. Eliot, W. H. Auden, C. S. Lewis, Flannery O'Connor, Thomas Merton, Annie Dillard, even Joe Coleman.

What do these geniuses find in Christianity? I believe that

they are drawn to the potent kernel of the religion, its abiding paradox: the more devastating the destruction, the more profound the redemption. The true source of Christ is the morbid.

In the summer of 2009, my wife and I traveled to Colmar, the capital of the French region of Alsace, and found ourselves in the Unterlinden Museum. There we stood, stunned, before Grünewald's Isenheim altarpiece.

In the center panel, almost nine feet tall, is the crucifixion. There is a creature nailed to a cross. The body—severely starved, with skin greenish gray and lacerated—strains. The head, tormented by a band of thorns, hangs bloodily, eyes closed, pained to blankness. The outsized hands clench like claws around the spikes.

To the left of the cross is Mary, Jesus' mother. Clad all in white, she swoons backward, disabled by grief, her hands squeezed in fruitless prayer. The supporting arms of John the Evangelist, who is clothed in red, save her from falling. Finally, to the right stands John the Baptist. He holds a Bible in his left hand, and with his right points to these words from John 3:30, hovering, in Latin, in the foul air: "He must increase, but I must decrease."

This is the bizarre ratio of Grünewald's portrait. When Christ is demeaned the most—belittled, diminished, and putrescent—he is the most expansive: noble, ubiquitous, pure spirit.

47.

Mel Gibson's 2004 film *The Passion of the Christ*, never backed by a Hollywood studio, was made with a budget of $30 million, paltry in the movie business. However, the picture grossed $370.6 million in the United States and almost $612 million worldwide. A primary reason for this success was the participation of Christian churches. Pastors bused their congregations to the movie and often encouraged their flocks to donate tickets to the general public, as a way of proselytizing.

All of this despite the fact that *The Passion of the Christ* is one the most brutal films ever made, essentially torture porn, with Jesus whipped and bludgeoned and stabbed and punctured for the entire twelve hours the movie depicts. In 2006, Gibson's film topped *Entertainment Weekly*'s list of all-time controversial movies, with Stanley Kubrick's notoriously savage *A Clockwork Orange* coming in second. *The Passion*'s grisly violence—some of which does not appear in the Bible—offended viewers and critics, including David Edelstein, who described the picture as "a two-hour-and-six-minute snuff movie." But the film was also scandalous because of its anti-Semitism. Its demonization of the Jews—the movie blames them for Jesus' death and generally portrays them as evil—agitated synagogues and antidefamation groups throughout the world. The critic Jami Bernard said the movie was "the most virulently anti-Semitic movie made since the German propaganda films of World War II."

Gibson's Christian gore fest is not unique. Around the time *The Passion of the Christ* hit theaters, Christian churches around the country were staging their own barbarous crucifixion dramas. In an article in *Slate*, Patton Dodd discusses the most prominent productions: the Memphis Passion Play, staged in Memphis's Bellevue Baptist Church; the Atlanta Passion Play, running in the First Baptist Church of that city; and *The Thorn*, first performed in the New Life Church in Colorado and now franchised in Minnesota and South Carolina.

These productions are, according to Dodd, "Bible spectaculars that would make Cecil B. DeMille swoon." The plays rely on "flaming swords, pyrotechnics, and barrel-chested bodies dancing, leaping, flipping across the stage, and swirling down from the rafters." There are angels battling demons. There are perpetually shifting images on a background screen, dictating horror or transcendence. There are crescendos of melodramatic music. There is outrageous violence: Jesus undergoes a vicious scourging with the cat-o'-nine-tails, thirty-nine lashes; he trudges battered and bloody to Golgotha, carrying his own cross; his actual crucifixion is apocalyptically savage, as harrowing and excessive as anything in Peckinpah. Dodd is troubled by the overemphasis on the violence, claiming that it is less biblical and more a satiation of "our culture's taste for visual realism."

After my experience of Grünewald's painting—a meditation on the necessary connection between destruction and transcendence—I wondered about Dodd's tone. Were Christians drawn to these passion plays out of a base appetite for titillation? Or was there something deeper, an understanding on the part of viewers that the macabre might open to truth, beauty, and goodness? Or was the attraction somewhere in between?

48.

In the spring of 2010, I bought tickets to the production of *The Thorn* playing at the Seacoast Church in Charleston, South Carolina. I drove there from my home in North Carolina on Good Friday.

My expectations for the play were not high. I assumed that it would be an unintentionally campy rendering of the crucifixion, with bad acting, worse costumes, and an atmosphere of inflated seriousness. Brought up in a small, rural Southern Baptist church, I had seen one too many productions in the Lord's house, always amateurish and mawkish, grounded more in holiness than aesthetics. I was also at the time negatively disposed toward mainstream Christianity (I still am), viewing most of its American manifestations as narrow-minded and self-righteous. Finally, I knew that contemporary Christian music would be part of the play, and I cringed at the thought of having to endure canned rock of the Stryper variety or the peppy sanctimonious croonings of a gaggle of Amy Grant wannabes.

I had my notebook. I had my tape recorder. I was serious about covering the event. But I was also ready to mock, relishing the satirical asides I'd whisper to my wife while the second-rate actors were belting out their lines.

Once we drove into the parking lot of the church where the play was being staged, the mockery commenced. The church was a classical evangelical megachurch, as much a sports arena as a place of worship. Milling about in the parking lot were men dressed as Roman soldiers. The costumes were pretty bad—*Spartacus*-worthy sword-and-sandal garb.

These men were in character. They strutted about, attempting to look imperiously cruel. In the lobby to the theater, there was more of the same. Men and women in robes, vestures, head cloths, and sandals moved about.

Sandi and I were led by an usher (from the twenty-first century) into a darkened theater, large enough to hold two or three hundred. We sat and waited. The place was soon packed. The audience was tense.

Onto the stage limped an old man: John the Evangelist. Between lame slapstick routines and corny jokes, he narrated the story of Jesus, from his birth up to his death. As he recounted the episodes, they were acted out, in dumb show, throughout the large stage. Occasionally singers on high platforms located in the background burst into songs commenting on the events.

Satan, bald, muscular, his torso painted sickly white, hovered on the margins, demons by his side. When the scene called for it, he sprang into action, tormenting Judas, tempting Jesus. Angels countered, either in the form of buff young martial artists or acrobats descending, by ribbons and hoops, from the rafters.

Horror film clichés, these devils were not the play's true terror; it was the torturing of the god. After Pontius Pilate condemns him, Jesus endures the compulsory scourging. He is tied to a pillar. A Roman soldier, flushed with sadistic glee, flogs him mercilessly. His back becomes a grotesque crisscross of blood. He writhes and collapses, is held up, beaten down again, over and over.

The crucifixion is more distressing. Jesus carries his cross through the audience. The crown of thorns punctures to the bone. Blood saturates his flesh. He staggers under his burden, stumbles, heaves himself up again. Once he reaches the stage, the Roman soldiers lay the cross on the ground. They force Jesus down onto it. They slowly and loudly drive the nails into his hands and his feet. The metal-on-metal rings with the horrid and chilling clarity of total pain. The soldiers then stand the cross upright. There is Jesus, caked in gore, his sinews ripping, not a man but an agonized and desperate gasping.

During the early parts of the play, I had been pleasantly bemused. I couldn't help but make fun of John's stupid jokes, the hyperbolic caricatures of evil, Jesus' efforts to look sensitive and blessed, the treacly Christian yacht rock (Hall and Oates gone evangelical), the little bits of bread the extras distributed to the audience after the last supper. I whispered jokes to Sandi, and she to me. We giggled silently.

But with the scourging, the fun stopped. What took its place, for me, was self-satisfied triumph. Yes, I thought, this is what I came for, a display of how even the most ostensibly peace-loving people, Christians, are deep down drawn to extreme violence, the bloodier, the better. This urge for the macabre is, as I suspected, lodged in everyone's core. Here is a play—so my mind's commentary ran—that should be firmly based on the Gospels, and the Gospels barely mention the scourging. The extended and gruesome attention to this event clearly means that the story of Jesus is attractive more for sadism than love.

Just as I was settling into this smugness, the crucifixion occurred. The visceral performance of torture, only ten feet from where I was sitting, ripped me from my aloofness. Exploitative or not, the episode moved me. I had never seen pain performed so intensely before, and the agony gripped me, pulling me into sympathy and then to empathy: I imagined as palpably as I could what it would feel like to be starved and dehydrated, bruised all over and cut to shreds; to have thorns lacerating my head and nails hammered into my hands and feet; to have my limbs strained to the point of rending.

I glanced over at Sandi. She saw me in her periphery, and, still staring straight ahead, said, "Whatever you do, don't laugh." I was going to tell her that wasn't my intention, when I noticed she was crying. I looked beyond her, at the people in our row. They were weeping, too, as was everybody else I could see.

We all knew the ending: a beginning. Minutes later, after darkness covered the brutalized Christ, a single beam shone on a deserted tomb and then appeared Jesus, unwounded and all clothed in white. Real fireworks exploded, and the auditorium, filled with people cheering, was flooded with brightness.

Once the show was over, I talked to audience members hanging around the lobby. Each claimed to be profoundly affected by the drama. When I asked about the extremity of the violence, everyone said that the brutality made the play more "real." In each case, I pressed, wondering why the play was sadistic at the expense of biblical accuracy. No one was troubled by this. Each reiterated that the violence, regardless of the Scriptures, was essential for making the Passion more authentic.

I was frustrated with these brief, informal conversations. Those whom I interviewed, I concluded, were drawn to the violence for more reasons than they were letting on. There had to be, somewhere among their pious desires, a hunger for gore. This baser instinct, I suspected, coexisted with the nobler yearning imaginatively to empathize with the suffering savior.

The violence certainly moved me for multiple reasons. On the most basic level, I was, I had to admit, titillated by the brutality. It gave me a physiological rush—increased pulse, tingly skin. Added to this crude response (making me little different from an animal) was one no doubt generated by my cultural inculcations. I had grown up watching violence on television and so had been conditioned to be stimulated by the conventions by which mainstream media packages savagery. The macabre moments in *The Thorn* drew from these conventions, making the play little more than a commodity. I was glad to consume the product.

The violence also whipped my emotions to high turbulence—another attraction. Fear was there, and pity, too, and an array of other feelings—remorse, anxiety, nostalgia, affection. The intensity was enlivening, and the aftermath, serene. I know it's a theory, and that theory and life are different—but I had my catharsis.

Each of these three impulses drives toward selfish pleasure: animal arousal, consumption of commodity, vigorous emotion and release. Another draw to the bloody Passion, though, was nobler, empathetic. The crucifixion's vividness, ferociousness, and ardor: these inspired a transfer. I felt the breathing of the Christ enter into my lungs, and I exhaled into his sphere my outrage and admiration.

49.

Dante once wrote, in a letter to a learned friend, about how best to interpret a text, his text. He refers to a line in his *Commedia* that cites Psalm 114. When the souls destined for Purgatory arise on the shore, they sing the psalm "When Israel went out of Egypt."

Dante proposes different levels of interpretation. If we look "at the letter alone," the meaning is literal: the Israelites, under the guidance of Moses, made an exodus from Egypt, where they were enslaved. But we can also understand the line on an allegorical level, as an image of the redemption offered by Christ. There is another level, too: the moral, in which "what is signified to us is the conversion of the soul from the sorrow and misery of sin to the state of grace." Finally, the line from the Bible can be grasped on an "anagogical" scale, in which it signifies as "departure of the sanctified soul from bondage to the corruption of this world into the freedom of eternal glory."

Dante's passage exemplifies what in the Middle Ages was known as the fourfold method for interpreting texts—mainly biblical passages but also literary ones. This mode was even taught in schools, where this little pedagogical device helped students remember the system: the literal teaches "history," the allegorical, "what you should believe / the moral, what you should do, / the anagogical, where you are going." So the literal points to events that actually occurred in time; the allegorical to an abstract system of theological, philosophical, or political beliefs; the moral to a principle by which one might live a good life; and the anagogical to a vision of the end of days.

Events are nuanced, and we react to them as such. Experiencing the Passion, I ranged from the most basic animal stimulation to higher functions of the human mind. Others in the audience, I suspect, had similarly layered encounters.

Not all events, obviously, are created equal: some call forth more complex, moving, and profound responses than others. Morbid happenings are especially lively in this regard, uniquely abundant, potentially sublime: moments that make us feel pain at our limitations, our ineptitude, our meanness; and pleasure over our expansions, competencies, generosity.

Morbid curiosity might be, on one level, "an enduring unusually strong attraction to information about highly unpleasant events and objects that are irrelevant to the individual's life." But it might also be compulsion toward grim happenings that are *relevant* toward one's life—that help one to manage dangerous fears and desires, to learn what is essential and what is not. Morbid curiosity is, on yet another plane, a *spiritual* yearning, a hunger to penetrate the most profound mysteries of existence.

In July 2010, I traveled to New York City with Sandi and Una.
I visited, one sweltering morning, the Ground Zero Museum
and Workshop, located at 420 West Fourteenth Street.

About fourteen other tourists and I waited on the street. At
the appointed time, a tour guide appeared and led us up to
the second-floor museum, no bigger than a typical living
room. Upon entry, we were each given a tape player and pair of
headphones, and then directed to sit around a wide-screen TV.
When told that we wouldn't begin for another few minutes, we
fell silent and stared around the white, brightly lit space. On
the walls were hung vividly colored photographs of firemen,
dirty and weary in the postattack wreckage. There were also
display cases containing artifacts—rubble from the Twin
Towers, including glass and steel; personal items found in the
debris, such as cell phones and credit cards; and what seemed
to be a piece, about three by three feet, of an airplane wing.

The guide told us that we would watch a brief video describing the nature of the museum; then we were free to walk
about the room as we pleased. There were about a hundred

stations, each focused on a particular photograph. With our headsets we could listen to commentary on each photo.

The video described the work of Gary Marlon Suson. From the instant of the first explosion until Ground Zero was closed to further searching, Suson chronicled in pictures the destruction and the struggles of those unearthing remains. His images were the ones now hanging before us.

Only minutes after the first plane struck, Suson rushed to the top of his apartment building—the building in which we were now sitting—and photographed the smoky billows sullying the autumnal blue sky. When he first entered Ground Zero after the attacks, he snapped the only part of the North Tower left standing: attenuated charred steel, all glass gone, a ghostly façade. His entrance into the buried subway station beneath the towers produced other images: a clock in the dispatcher's station stopped at precisely 10:02, the instant the second tower collapsed; a dented and windowless train car, beside which was a newspaper dated September 11. As days stretched to weeks and months, Suson photographed the rescue workers who dug tirelessly for the dead. One of these pictures is of an old ironworker. His face is slack, wrinkled, but resilient. He is taking a break in the middle of a frigid January night to smoke a cigarette.

The video ended. I looked around the room, trying to decide which picture to study first. I chose one of German shepherds searching for human remains. I pressed the number on the tape player. Suson told the story. When the dogs were unable to find bodies, they became depressed and lethargic. To rouse them, the firemen half buried themselves and played dead; when the dogs found the pretend corpses, they perked up. According to Suson, these shepherds were very good at their job. Now, sadly, most if not all of the dogs have died of the toxic air they inhaled as they pawed through the wreckage.

I next listened to the audio accompanying Suson's picture of the initial blast. After recounting his first minutes after the attacks, Suson tried to capture the first responses of others close to the horror. He played a tape of a Manhattan fire dispatcher mustering his forces in the immediate aftermath. The voice, a tension of professional clarity and desperation, announces the attacks and commands the stations to bring everything they've got.

That voice, old-time New York, with its brusque confidence cracking, upset me as an eternity of video footage could not. In that determined and despairing dispatch was a whole city's horror. I felt hot pressure behind my eyes. I was going to cry.

But I squinted, trying to hold in the tears, because somewhere, in the cooler precincts of self—those parts more mental, aloof—I concluded that grief is worthless in a merciless world, where mindless destruction reigns, where hatred razes towers: no place for love or longing. Why bother caring in this brutish colliding of carbon?

My absent daughter's face just then rose into my awareness, without my invoking it; I saw her in the Museum of Natural History, which she was then visiting with Sandi, and imagined her standing before an immense dinosaur skeleton. I *did* care, with all I had. I couldn't help it. And though I still did not cry, I tried to hold in my consciousness Una's sweet features, as a stay, however fragile, against the indifference.

I glanced around at the others in the museum. Some had swollen eyes, red and wet. Others were wandering around, stunned. Shuffling to the right, needing something to look at, I half stared at another picture.

I don't exactly remember the image—I think it was of a soot-covered fireman praying or of a clergyman blessing the mangled ground. I hit the PLAY button, and there was Suson's calm voice. I could feel my daughter's face sliding away, a purplish leaf on the brink of the waterfall, and then it did disappear, and before I could will it back, I heard what Suson was saying. As the search for bodies relentlessly lengthened and grief and fatigue intensified; as hopes coalesced only to be immediately annihilated; as firemen, bonded by their labor, grew close; as those who had lost their children and their parents, their wives and their husbands, realized, for the first time, the full intensity of their love; as all consumed by the wreckage brooded over death—as all of this was transpiring, the rescue work, according to Suson, became an act of worship, and this place a temple: "holy ground."

My tears streamed. I stepped back, wiping my eyes. I returned my audio set. I purchased the book containing Suson's photographs, *Requiem*. I walked to the hotel. When I pulled back the room's door, there they were, Sandi and Una, returned from the ancient bones. I lifted the book and placed it on the desk, opened it to a picture of a small plastic girl doll, arms gone, filthy and lonely amid the ruin, and pointed to it, and said to my family:

"Look."

BIBLIOGRAPHICAL NOTES

1.

An interesting paper on reactions to the events of 9/11 is "Why We Watch: Factors Affecting Exposure to Tragic Television News," by Cynthia A. Hoffner, Yuki Fujioka, Jiali Ye, and Amal G. S. Ibrahim (in *Mass Communication and Society* 12:2 [2009], 193–216). The authors found that those who feared most for their own lives as well as those of their loved ones showed very strong interest in the footage of the attacks. Perhaps, the authors conjecture, morbid curiosity arises in the face of threat: we are especially keen on witnessing violent events that might negatively impact our own lives. Certainly this idea accounts partially for my own fixation on the footage: I was terrified of further violence harming my unborn child. Another useful discussion of our attraction to negative news stories is "Effects of Morbid Curiosity on Perception, Attention, and Reaction to Bad News," by Kevin Pinkerton and Shuhua Zhou (in *The University of Alabama McNair Journal* 7 [2007], 129–43). The study concludes that physical arousal is a primary cause of morbid curiosity toward negative news stories: we are drawn to footage that stimulates our bodies, and violent images frequently give rise to visceral fear or anxiety.

2.

In *Staring: How We Look* (Oxford: Oxford University Press, 2009), Rosemarie Garland-Thomson emphasizes the intense physicality of staring—when we "rubberneck," we experience raised levels of dopamine and electrical activity as well as a faster heart rate. One source of this physical stimulation is psychological. In staring we are *straining* to understand what we are gazing upon. Also, we are reliving what Garland-Thomson calls the "primal scene of staring," that moment when our parents told us to stop gawking and thus set up the lifelong tension between our urge to stare and the collective condemnation of staring as rude. Of course, as Garland-Thomson points out, there are numerous motivations behind each act of staring. Sometimes we stare attentively, in hopes of helping someone who might be suffering. At other times, we gawk more maliciously, as when we take perverse pleasure in our alleged superiority to someone handicapped. At still other times, we experience "baroque staring," the irresistible gaze elicited by radical novelty. I imagine that much of our morbid gawking—at such events as traffic accidents and fights—combines all three: we empathize, we are relieved that we're not the one suffering, and we are simply stunned before the sudden eruption of the "out-of-the-ordinary." For an excellent article on Garland-Thomson's work, see Peter Monaghan's "The Gaze, Reconsidered," in *Chronicle of Higher Education* 55:36 (May 2009).

3.

The Gary Laderman quotation on the "separation of death from everyday life" is from his book *Rest in Peace: A Cultural History of Death and the Funeral Home in Twentieth-Century America* (Oxford: Oxford University Press, 2005), p. 3. The quotation from Philippe Ariès is from his *The Hour of Death*, translated by Helen Weaver (New York: Knopf, 1981), p. 586. Lyn Margulis, along with Laderman and Ariès, is quoted in Burkhard Bilger's "Nature's Spoils," in *The New Yorker*, Nov. 22, 2010, p. 106. Bilger's own quote is in the same article (p. 106). William Carlos Williams's phrase "The pure products of America / go crazy" is from "To Elsie," in the collection *Spring and All* (1923).

4.

William Blake once wrote, in his annotations to Sir Joshua Reynolds's *Discourses*, that "To Generalize is to be an Idiot. To Particularize is the Alone Distinction of Merit—General Knowledges are those Knowledges that Idiots possess." But this condemnation of generality is, of course, a general statement.

5.

Wordsworth's idea of "spots of time" can be found in his 1805 version of *The Prelude*, 12.208–18. I should note that my brother and his friend grew up to create a horror film of their own, an accomplished and very interesting one, with my brother Kirk starring and his friend, Onur Tukel, directing (under the pseudonym Sergio Lapel). The movie is called *Drawing Blood*, from 1999, distributed by Troma Entertainment, the company that brought us *The Toxic Avenger* (1985).

6.

The Poe quotation comes from his piece "The Imp of the Perverse," in *The Complete Stories and Poems of Edgar Allan Poe* (New York: Doubleday, 1984), pp. 273–74.

7.

The Haskins quotation is from his essay "Morbid Curiosity and the Mass Media: A Synergistic Relationship," in *Morbid Curiosity and the Mass Media: Proceedings of a Symposium*, edited by James A. Crook, Jack B.

Haskins, and Paul G. Ashdown (Knoxville: The University of Tennessee and the Gannett Foundation, 1984), p. 8. This collection of articles, based on a 1984 symposium at the University of Tennessee, is one of the few rigorous academic explorations of morbid curiosity. As Haskins himself claims, "It is . . . surprising that a thorough review of psychological and communications literature has failed to produce any research citations on morbid curiosity per se, not even a definition of the concept" (p. 2). Fourteen years later, in 1998, Dolf Zillmann, a distinguished professor of communications and psychology at the University of Alabama and a leading expert in media violence, noted that the situation had not really changed: "Given that our attraction to portrayals of violence and its aftermath is obtrusive in filling movie and television screens and books and papers, in both fiction and nonfiction, it is astounding how little attention psychologists have paid to this phenomenon" (*Why We Watch: The Attractions of Violent Entertainment*, ed. Jeffrey H. Goldstein [Oxford: Oxford University Press, 1998], p. 181).

Now, in 2011, in spite of the compelling research of scholars like Haskins and Zillmann, scientific work on our enduring fascination with the macabre is not nearly as extensive as one might imagine. I just entered the term "morbid curiosity" in the Web of Science database, a major index of scholarship in the physical sciences and social sciences. The search yielded only four articles that focus on the concept. Only two articles appeared when I used the same term to search the Biological Abstracts database, an expansive archive of journals devoted to the life sciences. When I entered "suffering of others" in the Web of Science, I got only twelve entries that home in on the experience of another's pain; my entry of the same phrase in the biology database returned no articles that directly address our witnessing of suffering. There's not even a Wikipedia entry for "morbid curiosity"—only a subentry for the phrase, under the heading "Curiosity." In this small paragraph, we fittingly learn that morbid curiosity is often likened to the "Train Wreck Syndrome" or "Car Crash Syndrome." Neither of these concepts gets its own entry, though, nor could I find any discussion of them in the scientific literature. Why have scientists largely neglected morbid curiosity, obviously a fundamental element of existence? Do most scientists slight morbid curiosity because of their shame over their own macabre fascinations?

This seems unlikely; scientists have always justly prided themselves on their ability to study the most putatively perverse parts of life objectively, indifferent to societal censure. Still, the lack of research on macabre fascination is odd, suggesting reticence in the scientific community, maybe squeamishness toward what most of us don't want to admit—we surreptitiously love looking at the outré. Many of the studies I consulted view morbid curiosity in a negative light, as Haskins does. Professor H. J. Eysenck, cited by Haskins, captures this prevailing negativity in a more direct fashion. "Morbid curiosity," he writes, " almost by definition, is a neurotic response . . . It might be found, for instance, in condition-avoidance responses which prevent a person from satisfying perfectly natural curiosity, and hence deflect this in unusual and unnatural ways" (*Morbid Curiosity*, p. 8).

I base my description of the macabre elephants on Iain and Oria Douglas-Hamilton's *Among the Elephants* (New York: Penguin, 1978), cited in Colin Beer's contribution to *Morbid Curiosity and the Mass Media*, "Fearful Curiosity in Animals" (pp. 51–89). The Douglas-Hamiltons and Beer alike consider the possible evolutionary value of the elephants' behavior, but remain inconclusive (*Morbid Curiosity*, pp. 59–67). Fourteen years after Beer's speculations, Dolf Zillmann weighs in, and offers more certainty. He claims that the morbid behaviors of animals—namely elephants, gazelles, and bonnet macaque monkeys—are not instances of macabre curiosity at all, at least not in the way that humans express it. Neither "prehuman death rites or expressions of death defiance," these weird zoological habits are, to Zillmann's mind, "easily explained as imperfections in maternal instinct and as the result of habituation." Elephants poking at corpses are engaging in "temporarily nonadaptive" behaviors; their instincts have for a time "gone awry" in the face of incomprehensible death. And the ostensibly danger-seeking gazelles and monkeys are really just used to peril, and so their "adaptive anxieties" have deteriorated (*Why We Watch*, pp. 191–94).

But a very recent article suggests that Zillmann's assuredness might be premature. In 2006, Karen McComb, Lucy Baker, and Cynthia Moss published a piece exploring why elephants are fixated on the tusks and bones of their dead. After describing the phenomenon, they confess that the habit might have evolutionary value but they can't quite ascertain what that is. They also wonder if the behavior relates to the death rituals of other species, namely humans. They encourage further study ("African Elephants Show High Levels of Interest in the Skulls and Ivory of their Own Species," *Biology Letters* 2 [2006], 26–28.)

8.

The Greil Marcus quotation is from "The Old, Weird America," in *A Booklet of Essay, Appreciations, and Annotations Pertaining to the* Anthology of American Folk Music, *Edited by Harry Smith* (Washington, DC: Smithsonian Folkways Recordings, 1997). This booklet is contained in the boxed set of Smith's *Anthology*, released in 1997. Marcus's essay is a work of art itself, as is his wonderful book *Invisible Republic: Bob Dylan's Basement Tapes* (New York: Holt paperbacks, 1998), which discusses Smith's collection in harrowingly lyrical detail.

9.

The quotation from Beer is from *Morbid Curiosity*, pp. 67–68. The macabre behavior of the elephants might in fact be less an example of animal instinct and more an example of a primitive sort of human imagination. As Beer conjectures, the sorrowful animals are probably manifesting what Julian Huxley has called "mentifacts," the mind's seemingly superfluous creations of fantasies, symbols, and myths. The macabre elephants, it appears, have imbued the tusks of their dead fellow species with special power. Doing so, they demonstrate a primitive, rather simplistic version of the "social intelligence of the sort from which human mentality might have evolved" (p. 72).

10.

Important proponents of the arousal theory—based on the idea that morbid curiosity generates especially intense physiological reactions—are Marvin Zuckerman, D. E. Berlyne, H. J. Campbell, James E. Fletcher, and Lewis Donohew. Haskins summarizes the research of Campbell and Berlyne in *Morbid Curiosity*, pp. 31–33, emphasizing how their views force a negative assessment of morbid curiosity. The views of Zuckerman can be found in his contribution to *Morbid Curiosity*, "Is Curiosity About Morbid Events an Expression of Sensation Seeking?" pp. 90–124; Donohew expresses his views in the collection as well, in "Why We Expose Ourselves to Morbid News," pp. 154–81.

The quotations from Maria Tatar are from her essay "'Violent Delights' in Children's Literature," in *Why We Watch*, pp. 70, 85. I follow the theories in that essay (pp. 69–87) closely throughout this section.

11.

The Gerard Jones quotations are from *Killing Monsters: Why Children Need Fantasy, Super Heroes, and Make-Believe Violence* (New York: Basic, 2003), pp. 6, 36. I follow Gerard closely throughout this section, mainly pages 30–36.

The information on and quotations of Maurice Sendak in relation to the film *Where the Wild Things are* come from Jack Shafer's article in *Slate* of October 15, 2009 (http://www.slate.com/id/2232550/), called "Maurice Sendak's Thin Skin." The quotation from Sendak's Caldecott acceptance speech is from Peter Hunt's *Children's Literature: A Blackwell Guide* (Oxford: Blackwell, 2001), p. 125.

Aristotle's famous pronouncement on catharsis, or purgation, can be found in Part IV of his *Poetics*. Here it is, in S. H. Butcher's translation:

"Tragedy, then, is an imitation of an action that is serious, complete, and of a certain magnitude; in language embellished with each kind of artistic ornament, the several kinds being found in separate parts of the play; in the form of action, not of narrative; through pity and fear effecting the proper purgation of these emotions."

12.

The Edison quotation comes from the *Edison Film Catalogue* 200 (1904).

13.

I take the story of Jung's near-drowning and "corpse preoccupation" from Frank McLynn's *Carl Gustav Jung: A Biography* (New York: St. Martin's, 1998). Jung very clearly lays out the three levels of the self in *The Structure and Dynamics of the Psyche* (*The Collected Works of C.G. Jung*, vol. 8, trans. Gerhard Adler and R.F.C. Hull [Princeton, NJ: Bollingen Press of Princeton University Press, 1970], paragraphs 749–95. A detailed discussion of the shadow, its relationship to other archetypes, and the importance of integrating it occurs in *Aion: Researches into the Phenomenology of Self, The Collected Works*, vol. 9.2, translated by Gerhard Adler and R.F.C. Hull, paragraphs 1-42. Jung tells the story of his crisis and how he healed himself through imagining his unconscious in *Memories, Dreams, Reflections*, edited by Aniela Jaffe, translated by Clara and Richard Winston (New York: Vintage, 1989), pp. 170–237.

14.

The quotation from Kael is in Jason Zinoman's *Shock Value: How a Few Eccentric Outsiders Gave Us Nightmares, Conquered Hollywood, and Invented Modern Horror* (New York: Penguin, 2011), p. 212. Zinoman's own quote is on page 213. The quotation from Guillermo del Toro is from an interview with Staci Layne Wilson in *horror.com*, on June 1, 2009 (http://horror .com/php/article-282-1.html). Morris Dickstein's line comes from "The

Aesthetics of Fright," in *Planks of Reason: Essays on Horror Film*, edited by B. K. Grant (Metuchen, NJ: Scarecrow Press, 1984), p. 69, quoted in *Why We Watch*, p. 188. W. H. Rockett's quotation is from *Devouring Whirlwind: Terror and Transcendence in the Cinema of Cruelty* (New York: Greenwood Press, 1988), p. 3, quoted in *Why We Watch.*

Rockett bases this theory on Antonin Artaud's theater of cruelty, which Artaud developed in his essay from 1938, *Theater and Its Double.* Artaud felt that most people are living a sham, erroneously believing that existence is good and just—that God's in his heaven and all's right in the world. Theater, he thought, could break through this "shroud over our perceptions" by revealing to audiences the true nature of life: it is cruel, a "tyranny," to quote Rockett, "of unpredictable, unfathomable forces that transcend the reasoned limits of reality as humanity understands them." To shock audiences into consciousness of these powers, the theater must generate "a series of shocks" (p. 61).

Another important source from which I've drawn for this brief discussion of horror film is H. P. Lovecraft's seminal essay on the power of the supernatural to open us to expansive mysteries: *Supernatural Horror in Literature*, introduction by Everett F. Bleiler (New York: Dover, 1973). The quotation from Aristotle on catharsis, already quoted above, can be found in Part IV of his *Poetics.*

The definitive source on the relationship between love and death is Denis de Rougement, *Love in the Western World*, translated by Montgomery Belgion (Princeton, NJ: Princeton University Press, 1983).

Stephen King on catharsis can be found in *Danse Macabre* (New York: Gallery, 2010), p. 210. Alfred Hitchcock on the same is in *The National Observer*, August 15, 1966.

15.

The Encyclopedia of Communication and Information, ed. Jorge Reina Schement (New York: Macmillan Reference, 2001) is clear on the ostensible erroneousness of the catharsis theory. In the entry "Catharsis Theory and Media Effects," we learn that "hundreds of studies have converged on the conclusion that viewing violence increases aggression." According to this article, the correlation between viewing violence and heightened aggression is only a tad lower than the correlation between smoking and lung cancer. Once she had studied the data leading up to this conclusion, top psychologist Carol Tavris in 1988 confidently proclaimed, "It is time to put a bullet, once and for all, through the heart of the catharsis hypothesis. The belief that observing violence (or 'ventilating it') gets rid of hostilities has virtually never been supported by research" ("Beyond Cartoon Killings: Comments on Two Overlooked Effects of Television," in *Television as a Social Issue*, ed. Stuart Oskamp [Newbury Park, CA: Sage Publications, 1988]).

For Frank Zappa's account of his battle with Tipper, see *The Real Frank Zappa Book* (New York: Fireside, 1990), penned by Zappa himself, along with Peter Occhiogrosso, pp. 261–92. Tipper's own views can be found in her 1988 book *Raising PG Kids in an X-Rated Society* (Bantam).

16.

In the paragraph on Noël Carroll, I draw mainly from pages 27–67 in *The Philosophy of Horror: or, The Paradoxes of the Heart* (New York: Routledge, 1990). Clark McCauley describes his study and interprets it in his essay "When Screen Violence Is Not Attractive," in *Why We Watch*, pp. 144–62. His quotations are from pages 161–62 of that article.

17.

Goya's painting first struck me when I saw it on the cover of Carroll's *The Philosophy of Horror*.

18.

The quotations from Burke are from pages 57 and 44, respectively, of his *A Philosophical Inquiry into the Origin of Our Ideas of the Sublime and the*

Beautiful (Oxford: Oxford University Press, 2009). For Kant's theory of the sublime, see *Critique of Judgement*, translated by James Creed Meredith (Oxford: Oxford University Press, 1978), pp. 90–203.

An interesting corollary to the horror of the sublime is the horror of abjection. According to the literary theorist Julia Kristeva in *The Power of Horror: An Essay on Abjection* (trans. Leon S. Rudiez [New York: Columbia University Press, 1982]), abjection, even if it intimates disgusting descents into inhumanity, is a mode of transcendence, an invitation to go beyond our tiny egos and encounter reality, a path, in essence, to the sublime. Kristeva asks why we yearn for the annihilation of our rational, social, familiar self, for death, and the worst of death: putrescence. The dead thing, inevitably rotting into a revolting cesspool and thus also evocative of sewage, reveals to us what we "permanently thrust aside in order to live." To maintain our sense of our subjectivity—our ego, our "I"—we must distinguish ourselves from the objects we behold and also from the materiality of our own bodies. The corpse reminds us, though, of the reality we labor to forget: we are object as much as subject, materiality as much as conscious mind. Witnessing the corpse, we are forced to imagine our own deaths, our own "thingness," our ultimate lack of a unique, unrepeatable identity—we are but one hunk of stuff among other such hunks. The corpse, then, pushes us to the border between life and death, human and inhuman. Both self and other, subject and object, human and inhuman; neither inhuman nor human, object nor subject, other nor self—the corpse breaks down meaning, exists outside of conception. It is "that compelling, raw, insolent thing in the morgue's full sunlight" that "no longer matches and therefore no longer signifies anything." It breaks down logic; it dissolves order. It is "edged with the sublime."

19.

An excellent discussion of the Lecter phenomenon can be found in David Schmid's *Natural Born Celebrities: Serial Killers in American Culture* (Chicago: University of Chicago Press, 2006), pp. 105–37.

20.

In this section, I draw from pages 1–30 in Schmid's *Natural Born Celebrities*.

21.

René Girard's theory of Jesus as scapegoat can be found in *The Scapegoat*, translated by Yvonne Freccero (Baltimore: Johns Hopkins University Press, 1989). For a more general discussion of Girard's theory of the sacred, see *Violence and the Sacred*, translated by Patrick Gregory (Baltimore: Johns Hopkins University Press, 1979).

22.

I first encountered murderabilia in Neely Tucker's article "The Dark Market of 'Murderabilia,'" *Washington Post*, March 6, 2008. I draw from her article in my discussion of Clark. In the paragraph on Dave Reichert, I am indebted to Les Blumenthal's "'Murderabilia' Are Hot Internet Items," in *McClatchy Newspapers*, September 7, 2007. For more on the legality of the sale of murderabilia, see David Lohr's "Murderabilia: Art or a New Form of Victimization," *aolnews.com*, February 13, 2010. The quote from David Schmid comes from Tucker's article. I also benefited from reading Hilary Hylton's "Cracking Down on 'Murderabilia,'" in *Time*, June 5, 2007.

23.

Rick Staton first came to my attention in Tucker's *Washington Post* article. For more on Staton, see the October 11, 2001, episode of ABC's *20/20*, "Into the Bizarre World of Murderabilia," and Julian P. Hobbs's documentary *Collectors*, produced by Christopher Trent and released in 2006. I interviewed Rick in his home in Baton Rouge on July 11, 2010.

24.

Oates's influential essay on serial killers is "I Had No Other Thrill of Happiness," in *The New York Review of Books*, March 24, 1994. Oates responded to my questions via e-mail on July 26, 2010.

25.

The first quotation from Gore Vidal appears in Gerard Irvine's "Anti-panegyric for Tom Driberg," from a memorial service that took place on December 8, 1976. I found this source on *The Gore Vidal Pages* (http://www.gorevidalpages.com/2011/01/index.html).

The second can be found in *The Concise Oxford Dictionary of Quotations*, edited by Susan Ratcliffe (Oxford: Oxford University Press), in *Oxford Reference Online* (http://www.oxfordreference.com.go.libproxy.wfubmc.edu/views/ENTRY.html? subview=Main&entry=t91.e2457).

26.

On Schadenfreude, see John Portmann, *When Bad Things Happen to Other People* (New York: Routledge, 2000), pp. xi–46. The quotation from Laura Kipnis is from *How to Become a Scandal* (New York: Metropolitan Books, 2010), p. 5. Another interesting work on why we are drawn to celebrity scandal, in particular celebrity suicide, is Alix Strauss's *Death Becomes Them: Unearthing the Suicides of the Brilliant, the Famous, and the Notorious* (New York: Harper, 2009). She claims that one reason we are attracted to the suicides of famous people is that we enjoy being part of a mourning community, expressing our sadness (or curiosity) with our countrymen or the whole world, relishing the feeling of " 'I was part of that, I was there' " (p. xix).

27.

I learned of the "Sudden Glory" exhibition in David Bonetti's article in *The San Francisco Chronicle* on January 22, 2002: "Falling on Funny

Times: 'Sight Gags and Slapstick' Show Reveals Humor in Everyday Mishaps."

28.

Here is the Freud citation: Sigmund Freud, *Jokes and their Relation to the Unconscious*, edited by James Strachey, introduction by Peter Gay (New York: Norton, 1990), pp. 5–142. The quotation on "altruistic punishment" is in Brian Knutson's "Sweet Revenge?" in *Science* 305:5688 (August 27, 2004), 1246–47. For a popular overview of the concept, see Maia Szalavitz's "Your Brain on bin Laden: Why Vengeance Is So Sweet," in the *Time Health-land* page of *Time Magazine*'s, website, issue of May 3, 2011: http://health land.time.com/2011/05/03/your-brain-on-bin-laden-why-vengeance -is-so-sweet/.

29.

The account of "John" and the phenomenon of war porn is in Olga Craig, "The New Tricoteuses," in *The Daily Telegraph*, October 17, 2004.

30.

An excellent account of these plays and their significance can be found in E. K. Chambers, *The Mediaeval Stage* (Oxford: Clarendon Press, 1903), vol. 1, especially his discussion of the Christmas beheading game in the medieval poem *Sir Gawain and the Green Knight*. See also John Matthews, *The Winter Solstice: Sacred Traditions of Christmas* (Wheaton, IL: Quest Books, 2003), pp. 94–97. Sir James Frazer in *The Golden Bough* catalogues numerous rituals involving the murder of a king or a god, sometimes by beheading. See especially his section on the beheading rituals in various European Whitsun rituals, chapter XXVIII, section 1.

31.

Jonathan Hayes's account appears in the "Second Opinion" section of the May 21, 2005, edition of *New York*.

The Coleridge quotation is from *Biographia Literaria: Biographical Sketches of my Literary Life & Opinions, The Collected Works of Samuel Taylor Coleridge*, edited by James Engell and W. Jackson Bate, vol. 7 (Princeton, NJ: Princeton University Press, 1985), p. 306. The description of photosynthesis is from *Lay Sermons, The Collected Works of Samuel Taylor Coleridge*, edited by R. J. White, vol. 6 (Princeton, NJ: Princeton University Press, 1972), p. 72.

Harold Schechter makes his claims about the importance of narrative for giving shape and meaning to horrific events in *Savage Pastimes: A Cultural History of Violence* (New York: St. Martin's, 2005), pp. 136, 157–58. He elaborated on this idea in a telephone interview with me in January 2010.

32.

I first came across the Hardy story in Blake Morrison's piece in *The Guardian* on August 2, 2008, "What a Fine Figure She Showed As She Hung in the Misty Rain." Michael Millgate provides an account of the event in *Thomas Hardy: A Biography Revisited* (Oxford: Oxford University Press, 2006), pp. 62–63.

33.

David J. Skal gives a fascinating account of the life of Maila Nurmi in *The Monster Show: A Cultural History of Horror* (New York: Faber and Faber, 1993), pp. 238–42. His description of her blending of the morbid and the erotic is especially noteworthy, as is his sketch of her relationship with James Dean. Skal also writes insightfully about the sexuality of the television show *The Addams Family*, on pages 281–84. It is Skal who quotes Astin on page 282.

34.

Wordsworth's poem "A Few Lines Composed above Tintern Abbey," from 1798, vividly exemplifies the importance of distance for the nature poet. The speaker in that poem positions himself so that he can appreciate the beauty of the ruined abbey without being too overwhelmed by its particular details.

35.

For my discussion of fight clubs, I draw on Michael McCarthy, "Illegal, Violent, Teen Fight Clubs Face Police Crackdown," in *USA Today*, August 1, 2006; and on Thomas Korosec, "Street Fight Video Horrifies Arlington," by the *Houston Chronicle*'s Dallas bureau, May 20, 2006. The Orin Starn quotation comes from the McCarthy article, as does the Chuck Palahniuk one.

36.

A fine print of Joe Coleman's "And a Child Shall Lead Them" can be found in *The Book of Joe: The Art of Joe Coleman*, edited by Katharine Gates, introduction by Jack Sargeant (New York: Last Gasp, 2003). There are two pieces of excellent analysis of the painting in the volume: Anthony Haden-Guest's "Joe Coleman: Art without Anaesthetic," pp. 24–29, and Katharine Gates's "Key to the Paintings," pp. 184–85. I draw my account of Mary Bell's life from these sources, as well as from Gitta Sereny, *Cries Unheard: Why Children Kill: The Story of Mary Bell* (New York: Henry Holt, 1999).

37.

I interviewed Joe Coleman on July 22, 2010, in his Brooklyn apartment.

38.

The quotation from Joseph Campbell comes from his *Transformations of Myth Through Time* (New York: Harper Perennial, 1990), p. 204.

John Keats wrote "Ode on Melancholy" in 1819. The Wallace Stevens poem from which the line on death comes is "Sunday Morning" (1923). The Dickinson line is from her poem beginning "A wounded deer—leaps highest" (1860).

The quotation from William James is from *The Varieties of Religious Experience: A Study of Human Nature*, edited and with an introduction by Martin E. Marty (New York: Penguin, 1982), p. 163.

For an excellent discussion of the idea of the memento mori, see Harold Schechter's *The Whole Death Catalog: A Lively Guide to the Bitter End* (New York: Ballantine, 2009), pp. 268–71. A good source for postmortem photography is Jay Ruby, *Secure the Shadow: Death and Photography in America* (Boston, MA: MIT Press, 1999).

The famous Yorick moment in *Hamlet* occurs in act 5, scene 1. Thomas Gray's famous elegy was written in 1750 and published in 1751. The line from Robert Herrick is from the poem "To the Virgins, to Make Much of Time" (1648), the consummate carpe diem poem.

Martin Heidegger develops his ideas on "being-toward-death" in *Being and Time* (1927).

Percy Bysshe Shelley's "Defence of Poetry" was written in 1821. The quotation can be found in *Shelley's Poetry and Prose*, edited by Donald H. Reiman and Neil Fraistat, 2nd ed. (New York: Norton, 2002), p. 517.

39.

I interviewed Nowell Briscoe in his home in Atlanta on June 24, 2010. I first heard of him on an *All Things Considered* segment called "Nowell Briscoe: Archivist of Death Revisits the Past," aired on December 28, 2009.

40.

Joshua Wolf Shenk's *Lincoln's Melancholy* (New York: Mariner, 2006) and Shelby Foote's section on Lincoln in volume 1 of *The Civil War: A Narrative* (New York: Vintage, 1986) continue to enthrall me.

41.

Richard Sharpley and Phillip R. Stone's *The Darker Side of Travel: The Theory and Practice of Dark Tourism* (Bristol, UK: Channel View Publications, 2009) is an excellent introduction to recent scholarship on thanotourism. Sharpley's "Shedding Light on Dark Tourism: An Introduction," pp. 3–22, was especially informative. Another helpful volume is John Lennon and Malcolm Foley's *Dark Tourism* (Florence, KY: Cengage Learning Business Press, 2000). Another good source is http://www .dark-tourism.org.uk/, which announces that their "dedicated academic research centre called the Institute for Dark Tourism Research (*i*DTR) is due to open in 2012 at the University of Central Lancashire, UK." For the "top ten" dark tourism destinations, some of which I mention here, see vacationideas.com at http://www.vacationideas.me/travel-tips/top -10-dark-tourism-destinations/.

42.

The quotes from Susan Sontag come from *Regarding the Pain of Others* (New York: Picador, 2004). The first, "snapshot of the little boy . . . if you will," is on page 119; the second, "the imaginary proximity . . . relations to power," is on page 102; the third, "initial spark," comes from page 103.

Martin Buber's *I and Thou* is to me one of the most lyrical meditations on love ever written.

For Stephen Dedalus's theory of the aesthetic, see *A Portrait of the Artist as a Young Man* (New York: Penguin Classics, 2003), pp. 206–16. All Joyce quotations come from this book: the first, "selfbounded and selfcontained . . . space and time," is on page 214; the second, "the luminous silent . . . enchantment of the heart," is from page 215.

43.

The quotation from Mother Teresa is from her posthumously published collection of writings, *Mother Teresa: Come Be My Light: The Private Writings of the Saint of Calcutta*, edited and with commentary by Brian Kolodiejchuk (New York: Doubleday, 2009), p. 230.

44.

This section draws heavily from my memoir *The Mercy of Eternity: A Memoir of Depression and Grace* (Evanston, IL: Northwestern University Press, 2010), as well as from two essays related to the memoir: "Mania, Academe, and Redemption," in *The Chronicle Review* of *The Chronicle of Higher Education*, September 26, 2010; and "Forgiving the Darkness," in *r.kv.ry. Quarterly Literary Journal*, January 2011.

The William Blake quotation is from *For the Sexes: The Gates of Paradise*, in *Complete Poetry and Prose of William Blake*, rev. ed., edited by David V. Erdman, commentary by Harold Bloom (New York: Anchor, 1997), p. 259.

45.

I interviewed Melissa Febos at a café in Brooklyn on July 23, 2010. The quotation from Kay Redfield Jamison is from *An Unquiet Mind: A Memoir of Moods and Madness* (New York: Vintage, 1997), p. 218. The quotation from Loren Rhoads is from *Morbid Curiosity Cures the Blues*, edited by Loren Rhoads (New York: Simon and Schuster, 2009), p. xviii, her collection of the best articles from her long-running but recently discontinued magazine, *Morbid Curiosity*. Additional material from Rhoads came from a telephone interview that took place in January 2010.

46.

An excellent source on Grünewald's morbid image of Jesus is Andrée Hayum's *The Isenheim Altarpiece* (Princeton, NJ: Princeton University Press, 1993).

47.

David Edelstein's quotation comes from his February 24, 2004, review of the film in *Slate.* Jami Bernard's is from her February 29, 2004, review of the film in the New York *Daily News.* Patton Dodd's *Slate* article, from which all of his quotations are taken, appeared on April 9, 2009.

48.

For more on "The Thorn," check out the franchise's website: http://the thorn.net/.

49.

The Dante quotations come from his "Letter to Can Grande della Scala," which can be found in *Critical Theory Since Plato*, edited by Hazard Adams (New York: Harcourt Brace Jovanovich, 1971), pp. 120–23.

50.

Gary Suson's *Requiem: Images of Ground Zero* was published by Barnes and Noble in 2002. Two powerful books on how compassion arises from suffering are Rebecca Solnit's *A Paradise Built in Hell: The Extraordinary Communities that Arise in Disaster* (New York: Viking, 2009) and Drew Gilpin Faust's *The Republic of Suffering: Death and the American Civil War* (New York: Knopf, 2008).

ACKNOWLEDGMENTS

I'd first of all like to thank the person to whom this book is dedicated—my brother, Kirk. He was not afraid to indulge his morbid side, and to revel in its wonderfully imaginative creations, when I was fixated on normalcy of the most boring kind. For a boy growing up in a small Southern town— rather backward, I'm afraid (the clichés are true in this case)—he fearlessly pursued his interests in weird comic book art (mainly the baroquely macabre images of *Conan the Barbarian*); wildly comical break dancing (Electric Boogaloo meets Devo), and, above all, horror films, from the cheesiest to the most legitimately terrifying. Even though I sometimes mocked him for what I saw as his ridiculous lack of cool, I secretly admired his outré, and very funny, energy. I enjoyed many fond memories of him as I traced, in writing this book, my own conversion to the macabre side.

I owe a huge debt to Harold Schechter, brilliant writer of true crime (see his *Deviant*, for instance) and equally brilliant scholar of the morbid (his *Savage Pastimes* is a good example). If it weren't for Harold's wisdom and generosity, this book would have remained rather anemic and academic. Back in January 2010, he agreed to a long phone interview, even though I was a total stranger to him, and in the course of our conversation taught me the value of the aesthetic in negotiating morbid experience, gave me a robust reading list, and listed others I needed to interview, including his two good friends Joe Coleman and Rick Staton. Over the next few weeks, he helped me set up face-to-face interviews with both Joe and Rick, who proved to be two of the most important presences in the book.

I am deeply thankful to Rick and Joe for agreeing to talk with me. Both were extremely hospitable, honest, interesting, and insightful—truly indispensable, and unforgettable. My evening with Joe in his Odditorium was one that will exhilarate and haunt me for years to come.

Another interviewee to whom I owe special thanks is Nowell Briscoe. The day I contacted him—soon after hearing his story on NPR's *All Things Considered*—he immediately invited me down to Atlanta to spend a long afternoon looking through his extensive, fascinating archive of obituaries and other memorabilia. As he led me through his collection, he entertained and enlightened me with powerful stories—some moving, some hilarious—about the mortuary arts, death, love, and loss. It certainly didn't hurt that we were fortified by the best gin and tonics I've ever had—and I've had many.

I'm also deeply appreciative to the great Joyce Carol Oates: she patiently and honestly answered questions that I e-mailed her, and, with her incisive and insightful responses, she quickly pointed out a major flaw in a primary argument and suggested how to rectify it. I followed her advice, and the book improved immeasurably.

Others generously agreed to talk with me, either by phone or in person: Alix Strauss, author of *Death Becomes Them: Unearthing the Suicides of the Brilliant, the Famous, and the Notorious*; Loren Rhoads, editor of *Morbid Curiosity Cures the Blues*, a collection of pieces from her recently discontinued magazine, *Morbid Curiosity*; Melissa Febos, author of *Whip Smart: A Memoir*; Greg Surratt, the pastor of Seacoast Church, a site where *The Thorn* yearly plays.

The book benefited mightily from important conversations with supportive friends I'm lucky to have: John McNally, Angus MacLachlan, Phil Arnold, Ken Cooper, Phil Kuberski, Dennis Sampson, Paul Bogard, Andy Lester-Niles, and Onur Tukel.

Yet again, I loved having Sarah Crichton as my publisher. She's a pleasure to work with—so supportive, interesting, and funny—as well as a brilliant editor, persistently, but gently, weaning me of my bad habits—academic obfuscation and purple prose—and encouraging me to vitalize my writing by using my own direct, clear voice. Sarah's assistant editor, Dan Piepenbring, was also a pleasure to work with. His suggestions were always right on, especially when it came to my attempted riffs on pop culture, and I also enjoyed a few e-mail exchanges with him on the artist now known as Prince.

Bridget Wagner, the agent for this book, was a wonderful guide at every single stage, from proposal to final draft. As always, it was a joy to work with her. I'd also like to acknowledge Dedi Feldman, the wonderful freelance editor who really helped me bring the proposal to life.

I also benefited from a story my dad, Glenn Wilson, told me, about a morbid experience from his boyhood and the dangers of going too far. He turned out to be an excellent interlocutor as I refined some of the book's ideas.

I deeply appreciate the ongoing inspiration of my mother, Linda Wilson, whose courage and resilience during a serious illness taught me deep lessons on the wisdom that can grow from suffering.

My most profound appreciation goes to my wife, Sandi Hamilton. From the time I wrote the first sentence to my placing of the last period, she helped me refine ideas, pointed out my blind spots, assisted me in my research (especially in New Orleans), and offered one of the best single suggestions I've ever received as a writer: Put the riskiest material at the beginning—in this case, my morbid fixation on the events of 9/11.

Finally, I'd like to say again how blessed I am to have such an exquisite daughter, Una, whose own quirkily comic morbidity keeps me laughing, and whose sweet affection saves me from going too far over to the dark side.

A Note About the Author

Eric G. Wilson is the Thomas H. Pritchard Professor of English at Wake Forest University in Winston-Salem, North Carolina. He is the author of *Against Happiness: In Praise of Melancholy*, *The Mercy of Eternity: A Memoir of Depression and Grace*, and five books on the relationship between literature and psychology.

CPSIA information can be obtained
at www.ICGtesting.com
Printed in the USA
LVOW11s2010270417
532434LV00001B/151/P